Why We Walk

Why We Walk

A series of stories, compiled by

Men Walking And Talking CIC

Published from stories of directors, walk leaders, members, supporters and invited individuals.

© Men Walking And Talking CIC

To Gentlemen, everywhere.

MEN WALKING & TALKING
EST. 2021

Why Men Don't Talk

Boys are told that real men don't cry,
So they hide their tears, and let their hearts dry.

"Man up," they say, and push fear away,
But the fear lingers, night and day.

"Stop acting like a girl," they warn with disdain,
As if emotions are something to restrain.

"Be a man," they demand with a firm, cold hand,
But the weight of this armour is too much to withstand.

"Men don't need help," is the lie they're fed,
So they carry the burden alone instead.

"Real men are providers," society claims,
Trapped in a role that only inflames.

"Men don't talk about their feelings," they hear,
So they bottle it up, year after year.

"Grow a pair," they shout with a sneer,
But inside, they tremble with unspoken fear.

These words build a wall, brick by brick,
Leaving them silent, making them sick.

In a world where strength means silence and pain,
Men are left drowning in an emotional rain.

Foreword by
Mark Ormrod MBE

It is undeniable that physical health, good physical health is intrinsically linked to good mental health, when you move your body, when you fuel it right, you're fit, healthy, strong, flexible and mobile contributing an unbelievably positive effect on your mental health because if you feel good you are good, you live good, and you perform good!

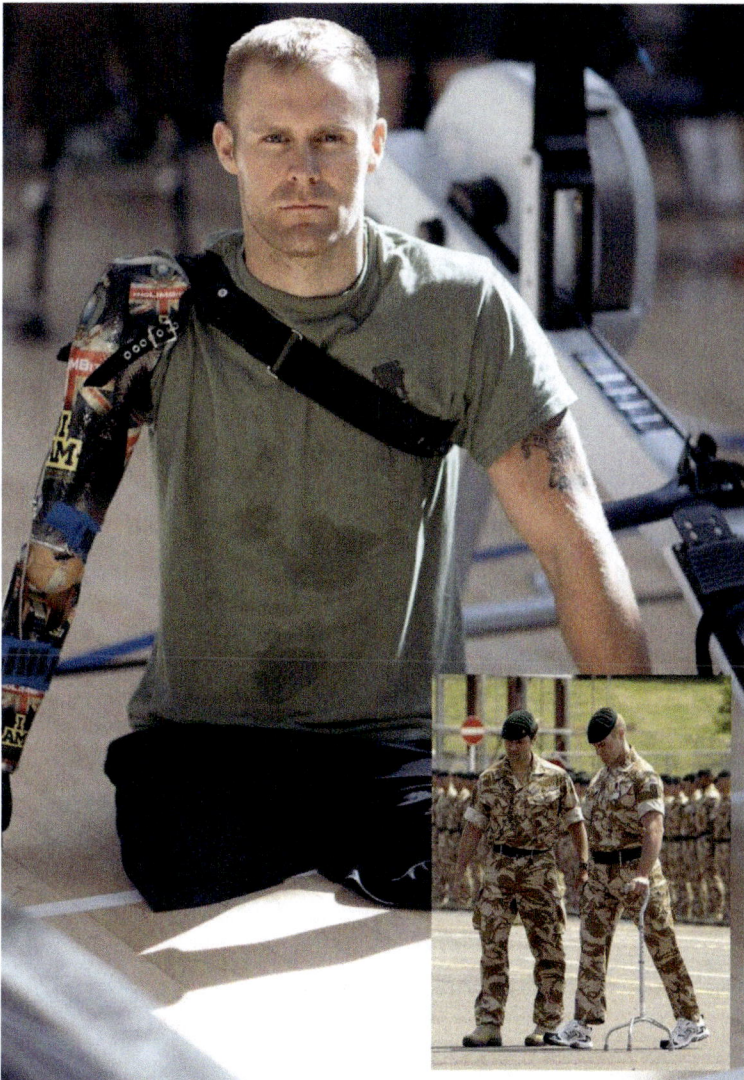

I always try to advocate to anybody who's suffering mentally just to get out there and move their body, it doesn't have to be anything crazy. I think a lot of people over think this and they think they have to run a marathon, as if it has to be a couch to marathon in three days, but to get the benefits is quite the opposite! My entire life has always been about small incremental improvements applied to consistency over time.

If you don't know where to start, or if you feel overwhelmed it's probably because it is overwhelming, in the past there didn't used to be any information out there about physical health and now there's too much, and it's contradictory a lot of the time so don't over complicate, don't overthink it, just get up in the morning put your trainers on and do whatever you prefer, go out for a walk or run for a minimum of 20 minutes, that's all you need to do and if you incorporate that into your routine, especially in the morning you're going to start your day off in the best possible way, you're going to have moved your body which is going to have a positive effect both physically and mentally which is going to have ripple effects and a snowboard effect for the rest of your day! When I figured this out I didn't know Id figured out.

When I was a teenager in the mid-90s, before the internet really existed, I was overweight and was bullied because of it. I started to train myself and I had no clue, I just lifted weights at lunch time in school and wanted to get muscles like most young men do at that point in their life what I didn't realize at the time, only realizing years later when I reflect is that not only did that make me feel stronger physically but after lunch when I trained at school I had so much more energy, I felt better, I concentrated more and it had a positive effect on my schoolwork! Normally I'd have been flagging, tired, lethargic and struggle against the rest of the day.

I found that everything that was happening was contradictory to what I had been taught and what I thought would happen if I were to work out at lunchtime.

I think I thought I'd be tired in the afternoon because there wasn't much research about the positive effects on mental health and mental performance. I believe anybody who wants to start some sort of physical regime needs routine, don't overthink it, don't overcomplicate it don't get paralysis by analysis and certainly don't research for hours and hours and hours, just get up in the morning put on your kit and go for a 20-minute walk and I promise you that if you do this and you do it consistently the benefits, both mentally and physically will be astronomical.

Talking is something that I'm big on and I try and flip the whole narrative on its head to try and get people to think a little bit differently. The stigma and the bullshit narrative is that if you're struggling mentally then to talk and to reach out and ask for help is weak! How can it be, because it's so hard to do and nothing that is hard to do can be done by a weak person, so actually it takes strength and a huge amount of courage to reach out and talk!

There is something I try and tell everybody that will listen, anyone that contacts me, whether struggling or not, the usual responses from those who have brought into the bullshit narrative that only weak men talk. When if you think about it, it can't be a weak person because if you flipped it into some sort of physical aspect it's like saying "Oh only a weak person runs a marathon". Can you imagine! But no, they don't because it's hard to run a marathon. it takes a strong person to do it and if they don't believe me if they don't think I'm qualified to give that kind of advice or that side of the coin then I always direct them to Foxy...

Foxy was a sergeant in the Special Forces, I dare anybody to call that man weak. He, along with the strong, courageous people in this book wrote down his thoughts, feelings, struggles, overcoming adversity, and was very honest and raw in reaching out and talking!

He talks so openly about reaching out and the help and support that he received, so if it takes a weak man, if it's a weak man that reached out and ask for help then I dare anybody to walk up to Foxy and say your weak as you ask for help, because I don't think that I'll end very well from the person that saying that to him!

Groups like Men Walking And Talking remove the ego from a man. If you said do "you want to tell me about your issues?" they would instantly be hesitant and they would feel all sorts of different feelings and emotions which would stop them, potentially going into defensive mode and walking away from the conversation. Flip that on its head and say "do you want to go for a walk?" and the answer would be very different! Subconsciously you are going out to walk, and talking becomes a by-product. These local communities in my opinion are a gateway to professional support for those that need it, and a fundamental assent to the local community.

A very similar example could be in jujitsu, I've been there before having turned up for an hours training and completing a five minute roll, then when we finish the next 55 minutes or just talking because they've come to that session thinking or it's manly, let's have a fight, rolling around choking each other and as soon as you at that fast five six minutes and their adrenalins up, the chemicals have started rushed around their body and brain, then all of a sudden they're inhibitions lowered and they start to talk. I feel it's the same with a lot of physical exercise, walking, cycling, walking or running.

Whatever it is, they're a gateway to opening up and talking, they remove those barriers and those inhibitions in a very healthy way. It's all about taking the first step...

We are proudly supported by,

Phil Vickery MBE DL

Phil Vickery MBE DL, The Raging Bull is a Rugby World Cup Winner, former England Captain, Celebrity Masterchef Winner and is a Mental Health advocate who prides himself with keeping himself both physically and mentally healthy. Over the last year he has supported Men Walking And Talking proving there is a need for these kinds of support networks. He is an inspiration to our members and supporters alike giving them the much needed push to attend our walks, helping to beak the stigma around men's mental health!

Contents

Chapter 1
How it started

Dan Reid
Founder, Men Walking And Talking

My name is Dan Reid. I am the Founder and also a Director of Men Walking And Talking.

Around 3 and half years ago I was in a very dark place mentally! I had no self-worth, no self-esteem and frankly said things to myself that I would not say to my worst enemy.

For months I was advised to speak to someone, go to therapy, get it off my chest but I couldn't summon the courage. It took me getting to the lowest I have ever been to take action!

When I eventually went to therapy and started saying and speaking about things that had haunted my mind for so many years I was able to start to find hope again. These conversations and articulating how I had been feeling for so long helped me to the realisation that I did not have to carry on down this path.

As I began to regain confidence I started to work with a Men's coach who has become one of my closest friends. Lee gave me strategies and asked me questions which helped me to think about why I devalued myself so much. I was then able to start to think about what I enjoyed and how it could give me purpose moving forward. From this Men Walking and Talking was born.

I started a small group in my community just outside of Telford in Shropshire. I remember putting out the first post on social media introducing the idea of MWAT, I was nervous and scared but remembered a quote I heard – 'fear is a mile wide but an inch deep'.

For this reason I feel I can speak from experience and a place of truth on my mental health in general. For years my brain lied to me, telling me that I was worthless and had nothing to offer, none of it is true. I speak to men regularly who have felt exactly the same way.

We all go through things in our lives that prevent us from being the person we should have been. The light, care free people we were before life came along. It is hard work but you can have those moments again.

The work I have done on myself has helped me to get to a place where I have been able to start an organisation that means everything to me. MWAT was started off the back of me seeking what I needed to improve my own mental health.

From starting a small group where I live to now having almost 30 around the country it has changed everything for me. The people who are part of MWAT never cease to amaze me in how compassionate, empathetic and committed to making positive changes they are!

Our Group Leaders who give up their time to hold space every week for men in their communities. Also our MWAT Directors who have become some of my closest and dearest friends.

Without 'taking the first step' and getting support with my mental health none of this would exist, I can honestly say it was one of best things I ever did!

If you need support it is available! Community and connection can change everything!

You are worth being well!

For Clem and Sophie

Chapter 2
Director stories

Mark Taylor
Director & Kenilworth Walk Leader

My name is Mark Taylor, I am 51 years old and started running a walk for MWAT on the 8th September 2022. Fast forward two years and this group has grown to regularly have over 20 men attend every week.

So, why did I start this group?

In early 2021 I realised I had a problem with managing my anger. This was something that had been a part of my life for a number of years but in true male fashion I ignored it. However, when it started to impact my work life and put my position at risk, I knew I had to face up to and deal with it. So I reached out and found a local psychotherapist and began 10 weeks of therapy. During this period I unpacked many boxes that contained events during my life, some of which were painful and upsetting but I knew I had to face them or I would never change my behaviour.

One event in particular was a serious car crash I was involved in in 1997, now, I have absolutely no recollection of the event itself and over the ensuing years I had recovered from my physical injuries and put in a box marked 'things that happened in my life'. Dealt with and moved on.
It turns out that this event had had more of an impact on me than I knew. After discussing it in the therapy sessions, I realised that I had quite a severe reaction to certain frequencies of noise; I would have feelings of anxiety, anger and sometimes even rage. I know this now; I understand it now and have the tools to deal with it immediately. But prior to unpacking that box I did not understand it, I had these feelings and emotions and did not understand them and they came out in the form of anger.

I know now that that event changed me as a person in a lot of ways, I now understand this and accept what happened and what it caused. I genuinely believe that now having addressed my 'boxes of life' I am a better person.

So to circle back, when I was asked if I would be interested in starting a MWAT group I knew immediately that this was my chance to give back and help in any way I could. Being a part of MWAT quickly became a passion and I felt the need to do more than just run a weekly walk.

So, in December of 2022, one of the proudest moments of my life was when I was asked to become a Director of Men Walking And Talking. I was presented with a role that allows me to follow the passion I have for improving men's mental health.

I have always been an outdoor person and as friends and family will definitely confirm, I love to talk. So being involved in a group that has those two things in the title, well it was meant to be.

My love of the outdoors and in particular, mountain walks, keeps me active in my down time, helps me to unwind and keeps me fit and healthy. My favourite place to hike is Cadair Idris in Wales, it is a magical place where I can unwind and reset my mind. Other favourites would include The Yorkshire Three Peaks Challenge which I completed in 2023 with MWAT.

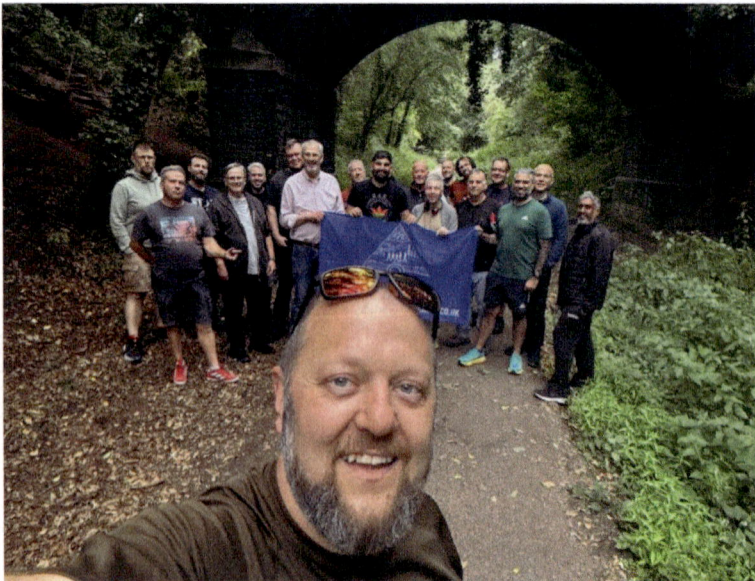

Andy Middle
Director & Shrewsbury Walk Leader

My name is Andy Middle and I am a Director of Men Walking And Talking and the walk leader of the Shrewsbury Men Walking And Talking Group. My story started as a young Soldier straight out of training and deploying to the Former Republic Of Yugoslavia with the United Nations. During my deployment I was part of the signal response team that would provide assistance and support when radio or telecommunications systems needed installing or repairing. During these duties we would travel the country and go on patrol carrying out peacekeeping missions which exposed me to the barbaric ethnic cleansing that was common during the war in Bosnia. On return to the UK, I felt psychologically effected but in the mid to late 90s mental health was frowned upon in the British Army and you would be classed as "weak" if you approached anyone to express your concern or problems. This meant that I had to hide my depression and the constant nightmares I was having due to the nature of what I had experienced on that tour and many more tours to come.

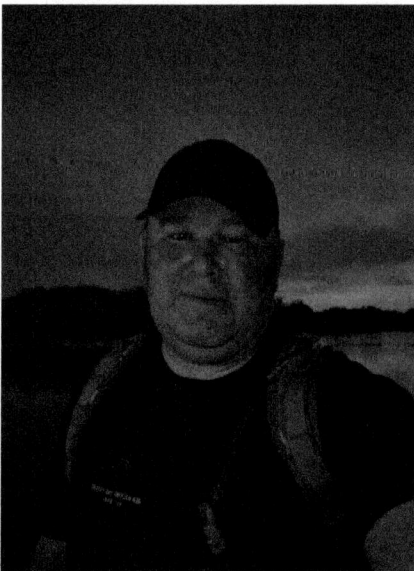

In the early 2000s I was injured whilst on operations and sustained a serious head injury that resulted in me spending 2 years in hospital 1 of which in Headley Court in Surrey. Whilst at Headley Court I learned to read and write, walk and carry out daily living functions that I had lost the ability to do due to my Brain Injury.

On my return to service, I subsequently deployed on further operations but unfortunately in 2007 I was diagnosed with Epilepsy due to my brain injury and was medically discharged in 2008. When I left the Army, I sought help from a mental health service, and they diagnosed me with PTSD and severe depression due to my service and brain injury. I began treatment with a psychiatrist and started to take anti-depressants to help me try and control the depression I was experiencing alongside therapy in the form of CBT (Cognitive Behavioural Therapy) and later on EMDR (Eye Movement Desensitisation and Reprocessing). After making good process I was discharged from their care in 2011 and using strategies I had learned from the mental health team I was able to self-regulate my moods with the occasional input from professionals.

In 2012 my Father took his own life after suffering from a mental health condition which saw me spiral back into depression slowly sinking into lower moods every day. Along with my Wife Faye's on-going support and Combat Stress I used strategies to lift my mood and stay happy enough to feel ok. In 2022 my wife saw a post on Facebook for a brand new men's mental health walking group in Shrewsbury and encouraged me to go along to the first walk much to my protest, even to the point that she drove me to the meeting point to make sure I went. The group I attended was Men Walking And Talking and apart from holidays I have attended every walk for the last 2.5 years becoming a Director last year. The group helps me in so many different ways including the "Brotherhood" I have developed with other members of the organisation whether it is men from my group or the wider group in general. It gives me a focus and helps me feel part of a team something that I think had been missing since I left the army.

The main thing is that helping others whether it is a chat or facilitating a chat really helps my own mental health because I go home after the walk feeling like I have helped others which in turn helps me. I attend every inter group walk that has seen me travel all over the midlands to meet other group members to walk around their local areas. I have taken part in the 3 annual sponsored walks we have hosted since the start of the organisation my first and favourite being the 3 counties walk that saw us walking 110 miles in 3 days from Chester to Worcester meeting other group members as we walked through their respective towns and counties. I look forward to watching the organisation grow and expand the geographical profile from north to south and everywhere in between because it works. Although the concept is very simple the effect it has on men's mental health and wellbeing is immense. I have seen it first hand and over the years with the guys who have come and go not forgetting the guys who turn up every week to support each other. I can also vouch for the effectiveness of the organisation from my own experiences of being a member and the positive effect it has had on my mental health and life.

"It's ok to not be ok"

Ashley Winter
Director & Hereford Walk Leader

Guinness world record holder, family man, always on an adventure, lucky guy who does so much, happy, proud veteran, charity fundraiser, career driven, always smiling and jovial...

If you asked anyone about me, that's the answers you would be given but in reality the hard hitting truth really is quite the opposite, how about depression, anxiety, twitching, huge emotional episodes, suicidal thoughts, adjustment disorder, feelings of failure, high pressured, unfocussed and unbalanced!

This is my reason, why I walk...

Since being a young child I remember going for walks in the country, playing soldiers, setting ambushes for the family, camping holidays and adventures and from what I can remember it was brilliant as I'm sure the wider family would agree that we wouldn't change a thing! It really is no surprise that I ended up joining the military, and following all of our adventures it was going the be the Army, although maybe not the regiment that was expected with dad being in The Parachute Regiment, but by far the best one I could have chosen.

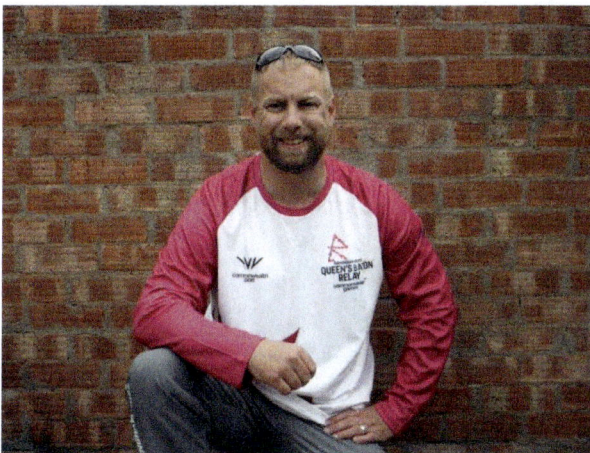

The Queen's Royal Hussars is the senior light cavalry regiment in the British Army although these days they use talks rather than horses but keeping those traditions in a ceremonial capacity reminds of our forefathers. I served for a total of 14 years in various capacities deploying on operations to the Middle East and The Balkans at the ripe old age of 18, it certainly was an eye opener.

One of my most memorable roles and one that has forged my path in a career and my involvement with Men Walking And Talking was actually in my hometown of Birmingham.

The Royal Centre For Defence Medicine, previously Selly Oak Hospital was a place where all military patients from around the globe were being treated, as you can imagine we had both low level and hugely complex patients and families, and for obvious reasons I'm not going to elaborate on. Being part of the welfare team really was a special role, an honour to be there to support those in need for a substantial amount of time, supporting individuals through probably one of the toughest times of their lives.

Having being diagnosed with Keratoconus and my vision deteriorating I made the move to a desk job and really enjoyed it, still in the military environment but having the flexibility to be able to continue to do a job I loved was the perfect environment however all good things do have to come to an end. Following discharge I found it tough to settle into civilian life, often thinking it may be better if I just didn't bother at all, finding myself on a 3rd floor window ledge contemplating what my professional life had become, I felt trapped in a meaningless job and didn't see a way out! Looking back, I often do, I feel it all happened for a reason and gave me the strength and knowledge to move into a new role as a Welfare Officer, back in the military environment supporting those in a similar position that I had been.

Since being diagnosed with Keratoconus, Anxiety, Depression and latterly Adjustment Disorder I found that so much support is available and have been very fortunate to be involved in so many events and adventures, mainly to test my Keratoconus and the limits of my condition to show others what can be done, that it doesn't mean things are over, but different, and for me different has been absolutely incredible!

Walking is good for the soul, it gives you the sense of freedom, a sense of purpose whilst wandering those trails, streets, mountains or tow paths, and it really gives you something to smile about. Walking is also great for physical wellbeing, even a mile a day can make you feel better no matter what speed you go and if you are anything like me then it helps with planning, having that time to think really is for the most part a positive experience.

I was asked a good few times by fellow director, Mark to join Men Walking And Talking as a walk leader but took time on the decision as I didn't want to do this half-hearted, I believe that if something is worth doing then you may as well do it to the best of your ability. After a couple of months I made the decision to join as a walk leader for the city of Hereford, starting in April 2023 I turned up for the walk alone for the first 4 weeks or so, enjoying the time to myself whilst also hoping the advertising and networking would pay off and someone would actually turn up. They say perseverance pays off and it did, week after week the numbers grew, some attend weekly, some monthly, and some every now and then but it's such a great community – members have helped each other get jobs, seek support and also meet socially proving this group is a huge success.

Whilst starting up my role as walk leader I was delighted to be formally invited to become a director, and am very proud to be helping run this wonderful organization and help it progress. In those 18 months I have grown the Hereford group, organized a family walk, a festive walk, an inter group walk and am currently planning more.

I urge everyone to spend time in the outdoors, you don't have to go far and you don't have to do it with us, there are so many wonderful places to visit in the UK and further afield, just enjoy and embrace it.

Chapter 3
Inspirational leaders

Dave Carter
Sandbach Walk Leader

My name is Dave Carter, walk leader of Men Walking And Talking, Sandbach, Cheshire. First walk started 01/10/2024

At 16 years old I joined the army, everything I ever wanted and worked hard to be the best I could. I started off at the army foundation college in Harrogate and quickly became a standout recruit. Unfortunately a snowboarding trip with the Army cut short my career and a medical discharge soon followed. But being a soldier taught me so much about resilience, teamwork, brotherhood, empathy, grit, strength and so much more.

I've worked a few different jobs over the years but as family life was coming in I started working at Bentley motors for that job security and career progression. I soon moved up through the ranks with my hard work and determination to learn more.

I progressed well at Bentley but it didn't challenge me and with that I started to get lazy and lose focus on what I really wanted from life. I came for the payslip and that was it. In 2023 I took redundancy from Bentley and now working towards getting my personal training and strength & conditioning coaching completed, finally getting back to what really drives me forward, helping others. I want people to find their best selves and support them through that.

I am married and have 2 amazing IVF babies that are my everything but the financial pressure of supporting my family is what hit me like a ton of bricks. As each month past, debt started to creep in and with poor decisions; it just got worse and worse. I reached out and spoke to a group of men and that really lifted the weight off my shoulders and helped me to see a clearer picture. I still have a lot of debt and I'm working through these problems I face, but I'm doing it on my terms.

I have wanted to set something up for a long time and coming across the Men Walking And Talking group was perfect. To me this is exactly what we need more of in our communities, a simple walk and talk can go a long way to building a stronger social connection and self-worth.

This is for every man.

Please join in...

Walk, Talk, Listen, Grow

Dominic Braithwaite
Cleobury Walk Leader

My first encounter with mental health struggles was in 2012 when one of my best friends called to tell me he had a breakdown. At the time, I had no idea what that meant. He agonised over sharing his struggles with us because, since our days at university, he was seen as the strong one—the friend we all turned to for advice. He feared we would now perceive him as weak. For me it was the opposite, I saw someone incredibly brave in opening up in an age where men didn't talk about their feelings. I saw first-hand how deeply his struggles affected him, like the time we went to pick up a pizza, and he was visibly overwhelmed with social anxiety. Despite witnessing his challenges, I remained under the naive illusion that my own mental health was stable and would likely stay that way. Little did I know then how dangerous and misguided that thought truly was?

Fast forward 10 years to the summer of 2022, and I was struck by my first real experience with anxiety and depression. The triggers were clear: a traumatic house move to a completely new part of the country, the stress of changing jobs, and the overwhelming task of trying to get my children into a local school. It all started to weigh on me, feeling like a constant, heavy cloud hanging over me that I couldn't shake off. Everything I used to enjoy felt hollow, and I had no desire to engage with anything or anyone. Even basic communication became a burden, and I found myself retreating further into myself.
It was particularly heart-breaking when it came to my family. I felt so disconnected that I had to set a 10-minute timer just to force myself to play with my boys, which made me feel even more trapped in my own mind. Suicidal thoughts fleetingly entered my mind. I sought therapy in hopes of getting some relief, but it didn't seem to reach the root of my struggles. The darkness persisted, and I never truly bounced back from it.

Less than a year later, everything came to a head. I broke down at work, completely overwhelmed by the mounting pressure I'd been carrying for so long. I knew I needed help, so I booked an emergency mental health appointment with my doctor. That led to being prescribed medication and gaining access to NHS CBT therapy. This time, the therapy proved much more effective. It gave me practical tools, like reframing my thoughts, which helped me manage the anxiety in a way I hadn't been able to before. Though I'm still on my journey, these strategies have given me a much-needed lifeline.

In the midst of my breakdown, the pressures of working full-time and moving to a new area compounded my feelings of isolation and loneliness. The move had left me disconnected from friends and support systems, making it difficult to form new connections in an unfamiliar place. It was a bad combination, especially for a man, where societal expectations can make it harder to reach out or admit vulnerability.

I remember one day, in a service station toilet, I saw a flyer advertising Men Walking And Talking groups. Something about it resonated with me, so I took a photo of it (carefully avoiding including any unsuspecting men in the shot), shared it with my wife, and promptly forgot about it. A few months later, while scrolling through my phone, the picture resurfaced. It sparked my interest again, and this time I Googled the groups. There were a couple of walks about 25 minutes away, but nothing in my immediate area.

My wife, always supportive, suggested that I start a group here in Cleobury Mortimer. It took me a few months to muster the courage to take action, but eventually, I reached out to Dan, a key contact for the groups. He mentioned that someone else, Greg, had the same idea. When I contacted Greg, his knowledge proved invaluable—he knew the best day to hold the walk and, as a keen walker, had plenty of local routes in mind. Finally, on Thursday, June 13th, 2024, we launched the Cleobury Mortimer Men Walking And Talking group with six of us. Now, we regularly have around five people joining each week, providing a space for men to connect, share, and support each other through the simple act of walking and talking.

What I love most about the Cleobury Mortimer Men Walking And Talking group is the genuine sense of connection and openness it fosters. There's something unique about the physical act of walking side by side with someone, rather than sitting face to face.

It reduces the intimidation of opening up, making it easier to share feelings or experiences that might otherwise feel too vulnerable. I think this has been incredibly beneficial for the men who attend, as it creates a safe, judgment-free space where we can be ourselves without the pressure to have everything figured out. The simple act of walking in nature seems to relax everyone, easing us into conversations that might be difficult in other settings. Whether we're discussing life's challenges or chatting about everyday things like motorbikes, we all leave the walk feeling a bit lighter. There's a shared sense of camaraderie, and I believe it has helped many of us realise we're not alone in our struggles. This simple, regular connection has been incredibly comforting and empowering for all of us.

For me personally, the Men Walking And Talking group has been a lifeline during a time when I felt isolated and overwhelmed. Moving to a new area, dealing with work stress, and trying to balance everything left me feeling disconnected and unsure of where to turn. The act of walking side by side with other men, without the pressure to be vulnerable in a face-to-face setting, made it easier for me to open up about my own struggles with anxiety and loneliness. These walks have given me a space to release the mental weight I'd been carrying, and the camaraderie has reminded me that I'm not alone in my journey. Sharing my experiences with others and hearing their stories has not only helped me process my own emotions but also allowed me to regain a sense of belonging and purpose that I had been missing for a while. It's been a simple yet profound way for me to reconnect with myself and with others.

The walks have given me the opportunity to explore the local area in a way I never had before. Through these walks, I've discovered beautiful countryside around Cleobury Mortimer—hidden bridges, tranquil streams, and old houses I never knew existed. Members of the group who have lived here for over 20 years have introduced me to the fascinating local history, which has deepened my connection to the area. My favourite walks are the ones where we climb a hill and get to look down on the whole town, including our meeting point, the famous church with the twisted spire. It's a simple pleasure, but standing there, taking in the landscape, makes me feel more rooted in the place I now call home.

As part of my healing from my breakdown I found the power of poetry really helped. Writing poetry has been a powerful outlet for my mental health, particularly when it comes to releasing negative thoughts. It allows me to express emotions I might otherwise bottle up, transforming feelings of anxiety, stress, or self-doubt into something tangible and creative. Through poetry, I've found a safe space to explore these thoughts without judgment, helping me to process and make sense of them.

Gareth Williams
Oswestry Walk Leader

I Joined the Oswestry Men Walking And Talking group back in 2021 not long after it started. My wife shared the group to me via messenger and said I should take a look. At the time but not known by myself, my dad's 20 year battle with Parkinson's was slowly coming to an end. I had struggled for many years with his diagnosis but Parkinson's just became part of our families' normal lives not realising how it was really affecting me. On joining the group, I realised that i wasn't the only son/man feeling the way I did and discovered that one of the walking group members had been through a similar experience a few years prior. Being able to talk about how I was feeling was such a release and it allowed me to start to process the years of hurt and pain i had been feeling. Dad passed away in 2022 but I kept walking every week as our group had become part of my weekly routine and i looked forward to seeing the guys.

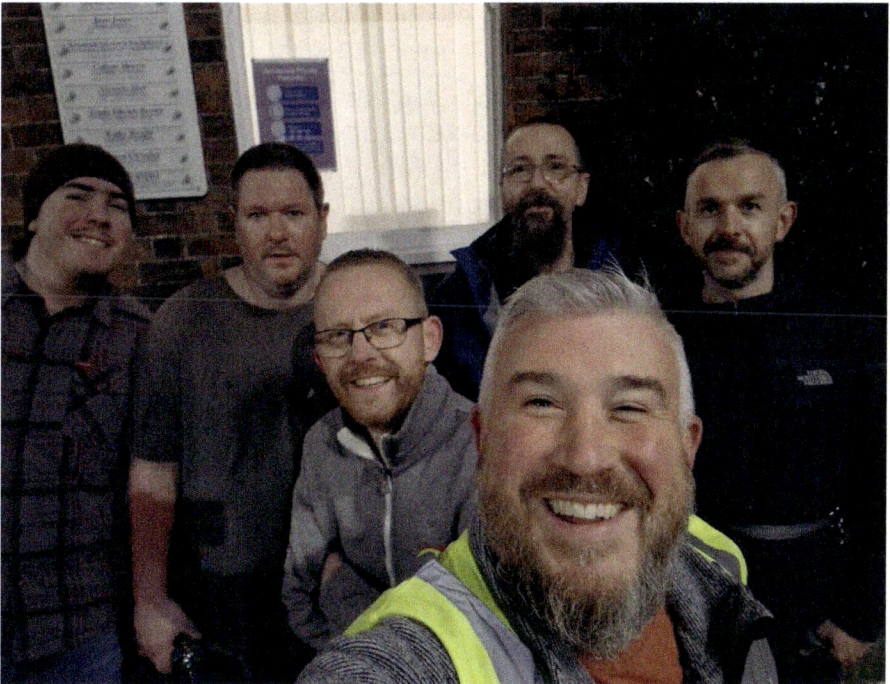

About twelve months ago the opportunity arose for me to take the position of group leader, i didn't have to think to long about it as i thought how much the group had supported me through the last year of dad's life and the grieving process afterwards. I wanted the group to continue to reach out and support other men by being there for them and that there were probably other men struggling with similar feelings as myself without anyone to talk to, I have amazing family and friends which I'm so thankful for but as life is busy for all of us, trying to find time with them is a challenge at the best of times.

The Men Walking and Talking allows me to have that one hour a week to myself in which I am surrounded by a group of like-minded men. The group have been involved in numerous community events supporting local charities and we continue to look for ways we can help locally as a group as it is really rewarding to do and gives a sense of purpose, Our little group consistently shows up week after week for each other and for potential new walkers, sometimes there's 4 of us other weeks there's double figures but numbers don't matter it's all about being there for each other.

I hope the group will continue to grow from strength to strength as I feel it's so important for men to be able to talk openly and honestly about their feelings and have a safe space to do so without any judgement.

Greg Ward
Telford Walk Co-Leader

Who you are....
My name is Greg and I'm 31 years old. I am originally from Sale in Greater Manchester. I moved to Telford to live with my girlfriend, Leia. I am a Support Worker who works with children and young people with additional needs.

Background information....
As previously mentioned, I grew up in Sale where I lived with my mum and two older brothers. I had a lovely upbringing and was close to my grandparents too. Sport was a key part of my childhood as I loved to play football and I support Manchester United.

The secondary school I went to often had players from Manchester United's Academy there so I walked the corridors with the likes of Paul Pogba and Jesse Lingard. I went on to study a degree in Coaching and Sports Development. Around this time, I started to struggle with my mental health and I took some time out to get the support I needed. Finishing that degree is one of my biggest achievements.

Injuries, background and MI's...
My mental health was stable up until 2021. My mum had passed away and I found myself in a job that didn't align to my values. I took time out, got support and was diagnosed with PTSD and Psychotic Depression. A year later, I was diagnosed with autism. This was a lot to take in but many things from my past started to make sense.

Why did I join MWAT (Men Walking And Talking)?
In 2021, my girlfriend saw Men Walking And Talking posted on Facebook. My love of walking had grown during the Covid lockdowns so this seemed like the perfect group for me. I wanted a safe space to share my worries and to make some friends. Although I found it difficult at first, the support I received enabled me to work my way up to a co-leader.

Favourite walks...
Growing up, the place I found that my father and brother particularly loved was the Edge walk in Cheshire near Alderley Edge. When in Sale, I would walk around the river Mersey.
Now I live in Telford, I enjoy walking around Telford Town Park with the Men Walking And Talking group. Some of my favourite walks are linked to the Silkin way. One part I like is Wellington to Dothill then through Dothill nature reserve and then through Bratton and back. I love being in and around nature and listening to music while I walk.

What I get from the walks each week...
I see the camaraderie and the healing which happens on the walks each week. I try my best to welcome each new member in and make them feel just as welcome as I did under our previous leader Simon. I now understand that we all have a different recovery path and it isn't linear. Some do it with reading, some find a listening ear, it could a game or a TV show that a friend recommends. Each member from the walk is unique and I am very proud of every member, past and present. Men Walking And Talking inspires me every day.

Future aspirations...
I have own a home, I'm in a stable relationship and I am in a new career which is very rewarding. I want to keep building myself up and other men on the walks.

Mahmut Yusuf (Mike)
Abbey Wood Walk Leader

Walking Towards Healing: A Journey of Male Mental Health and Wellbeing

Hello, my name is Mahmut (Mike), and I am the walk leader for the Abbey Wood group in Southeast London.

At 58, I bring a lifetime of personal and professional experience to my role as a Life Coach, Therapeutic Counsellor, and Hypnotherapist. Each walk I lead offers more than physical activity; it's a space for men to connect, share, and redefine their understanding of strength. The path that led me to this role is deeply personal and filled with lessons about vulnerability, resilience, and the importance of emotional support.

The Unspoken Burden

In 2004, life took a turn that I wasn't prepared for. My then-wife was diagnosed with breast cancer. The statistics were harsh—she had a 72% chance of surviving the next ten years following an intense regimen of surgery, chemotherapy, and radiotherapy. At the time, we had two young sons, just 6 and 4 years old. While charities and medical teams were focused on supporting her, I quickly realised that there was no real support for me. As a husband and father, I was expected to be the "rescuer," the "fixer."

I didn't have a space to express my own fears or vulnerabilities. The emotional toll was immense, but there was no outlet, no permission, for me to show weakness.
I vividly remember the one time I cried. Overwhelmed with fear and anxiety for the future, I broke down in front of my wife. Her response, though understandable in her moment of pain, was devastating: "Why are you crying? You will enjoy your life. Real men don't cry." Those words stuck with me for years, reinforcing a societal narrative that I had to suppress my emotions, hold them together, and carry on. I am pleased to say that my wife survived and is still with us today, but the emotional isolation I experienced during that time stayed with me.

Stepping into a New Role

Two years later, in 2006, I found a new way to give back to society—by becoming a school governor. It began as a way to support my children through their education but quickly became a moral duty. I wanted to make sure that the support and guidance I didn't always have growing up were available to other young people. My business was thriving, which allowed me to focus my time and energy on my family and community, particularly during my wife's illness.
As the secondary school became a lead academy, I took on the role of mentoring young male adults. Many of these young men were struggling without positive male role models at home, vulnerable to gang recruitment and the toxic masculinity that comes with it. I saw, up close, how the lack of emotional support and societal pressure to be "strong" was failing these boys. It was here that I first began to truly understand the crisis in male mental health and the urgent need for change.

The Turning Point

In 2020, my marriage ended. After years of loyalty, caregiving, and emotional sacrifice, I found myself isolated once again, this time judged for leaving my marriage. I was socially ostracised and confronted with the harsh reality that support systems for men, especially men in emotional distress, were severely lacking. This experience revealed the deep-rooted societal perception that men don't need help, that men don't cry, and that men don't suffer from abuse or isolation. I searched for support, but it was elusive. Part of the problem was a lack of proper signposting to services. Local health authorities and central government funding for men's mental health was limited, and societal attitudes weren't helping. There was a persistent belief that men didn't need mental health support, or worse, that admitting they did was a sign of weakness. I battled through bouts of depression, often feeling lost, but I came out stronger. Through introspection and my work as a therapist, I developed the resilience I needed to heal and help others do the same.

A New Chapter: Supporting Men on Their Journey

My journey brought me to a new realisation: "It's ok for men to cry or need help." This simple statement has become a guiding principle in my life and my work. As a therapist and now a walk leader, I create spaces where men can be vulnerable without judgment. On our walks, we don't just move our bodies; we move through our emotions, fears, and struggles. We talk openly, listen, and support one another in redefining what it means to be a man.

For too long, men have been burdened by societal expectations of stoicism and invulnerability. The result has been tragic—rising levels of depression, isolation, and even suicide among men. I've seen it first-hand and know these walks and conversations are part of the solution.

Walking Towards Change

Today, I strive to challenge the toxic norms that dictate men must always be strong, silent, and stoic. It's a slow process, but I believe we are making progress. Each walk I lead in Abbey Wood represents another step towards a world where men can openly express their emotions without fear of judgment or ridicule.

If my journey has taught me anything, strength doesn't come from suppressing our feelings but from acknowledging them. By walking together—both literally and figuratively— we can create a space where men feel safe, supported, and seen for who they are. I invite you to join us on one of these walks. Together, we can redefine what it means to be a man, one step at a time.

Conclusion

My story is one of pain, growth, and transformation. It reminds me that men, too, need help, understanding, and emotional connection. Through my work as a walk leader and therapist, I aim to provide that for others. I've learned that it's okay for men to cry, ask for help, and be vulnerable. It's OK to redefine what strength truly means.

Scott Grover
Barnet Walk Leader

Hi! My name is Scott Grover and I'm a walk leader for Men Walking And Talking, and have been doing this for just a few months now. I run a walk in Barnet, North London, which is a picturesque old English village that got swallowed up by London in its post war expansion, and so provides some fantastic scenery for walks. I am a recently qualified hypnotherapist, just beginning my counselling course, and heard about MWAT and the National Counselling and Psychotherapy Society's annual conference. I am no stranger to mental health issues, as teenage lad in the late 80's and 90's during the height of the AIDS panic struggling to come to terms with being gay in a far-right household of a conservative Christian family I was almost destined to have to deal with this, spending most of my formative years suicidal. Add to that I had an alcoholic father that was barely in my life.

I managed to push through most of my trauma and genuinely thought that I had dealt with it. With my therapist studies I have begun to realise that while I had dealt with it, pushing it down and getting on with life probably wasn't the healthiest of ways to do so, but through most of my life that's all I had. While I was never an addict or alcoholic, I have definitely abused those substances in order to self-medicate that internalised trauma. Because of my experiences I am very much aware of the need to have someone to talk to, I know the need for a non-judgmental safe space, I know the loneliness and isolation that comes from not having that, and with MWAT I can help provide that space for others.

During that NCPS conference I was inspired by Mark's presentation and absolutely felt it was something I wanted to be a part of. I knew it was something that was so desperately needed not only in my area but everywhere and so I got in contact and initiated the process of starting up a walk in my local area. And as great and satisfying as that has been that's really been just a small part of my MWAT journey. Since joining MWAT I have met some of the most amazing and inspiring men, and the group of walk leaders have become like family to me. I may not be the most active in our group chat but with my ups and downs of starting this new walk they have shown such amazing support and lent me their strength. I have been privileged to have been involved in promo work for MWAT and got to meet some of directors, get to know them better and meet some inspiring guys from other organisations. I don't know where this walk will take me but I know that this group of men have profoundly impacted the course of my life's journey and will be forever grateful for the strength, love and support this band of brothers has been to me.

Andrew Richards
Telford Walk Co-Leader

Housekeeping.

Our walks usually last between 45-60 minutes (the lighter/warmer months the walks are longer but usually it is a steady pace and is 2-3 miles long). We usually say dress and equip yourself as you see fit (bring water/hot drink, wear appropriate walking footwear and waterproof clothing/wear sunscreen/bring inhaler/high-vis jackets/head and manual torches etc.) Our Groups are open to Men 18+ (and their dogs). We have a strict no alcohol and no drug policy. There are no registration documents and no fees for us, but the public car park does charge £1.00.

Who we are?

Telford Branch of 'Men Walking And Talking' (MWAT). We meet every Friday 19:00 at the bench opposite TGI Friday's restaurant in Southwater, Telford Town Centre (except if unsafe to do so). We tend to leave at 19:05 to allow men a few additional minutes in case of delays due to traffic/finding a car park space / anxiety to attend our walks especially for the first time.

I am co-lead for Telford. I joined MWAT as it appeared on my Facebook and started to follow the group. I wondered if it were something that would benefit me and something I would like to be part of. I saw that men turned up despite poor weather. I then decided to as our slogan says, 'take that first step'. Even after a few slightly reluctant Friday walks, I started to attend our associated Tuesday night zoom: week 1: camera off and stayed silent, week 2: camera on and stayed silent and week 3: camera on and spoke. I Encouraged by MWAT leaders/curator Daniel Reid, to routinely attend the walk, I become its Deputy (then Co-Leader). Flattered that they had faith in me at such an early stage of my MWAT and Mental Health journey, I agreed. A previous work colleague described me joining MWAT as 'right up my street'.

I have enjoyed giving more than forty different men (so far) a safe space to be / to speak if they so wish/when they are ready. At the time of writing, we have reached a (joint) Telford record of fifteen men, sometimes we have had just one person, but a walk has still taken place and there is still photo evidence. I liked that the group has naturally evolved with both Greg and I as co-leaders and experienced members of the group (especially those who have preceded our involvement) will use social media / leaflets / our flag to promote the Group.

Similarly, family members, local businesses and colleagues are also keen to support us with donations/stocking our leaflets and our message goes further with their in-put.
We have a squad of regulars, who make it more times than they do not but if you are new, they/we will make you feel welcome, and we hope that become a regular member if that suits you. I love that it is free and if you do not wish to be in our in-walk photo: you can take our picture instead. There is an optional Telford only WhatsApp group 'Telford walkie-talkies' for members to reach out between walks/to advise if they cannot attend that evenings walk or notify us if they are running late.

I am grateful for the opportunities 'Men Walking and Talking' have given me: video for 'Mental Health Awareness' Group in May 2023, writing testimonies for our Facebook page/website, plugging our Merchandise and fundraising events, incorporating my MWAT in three work BLOGS, attending many 'World Suicide Prevention and Awareness Days', participating in walks of various lengths and degrees of difficulty, meeting so many like-minded non-judgmental men. I take pride and confidence when Daniel asks me to do something that he thinks I can do (like hosting our Tuesday zoom on one occasion), but he also gives me chance to say no, if I do not feel comfortable or ready. I appreciate when people have commented that they like what I/we do with the walks, changing and saving lives. Being part of other people's growth/development/ healing/Mental Health Journey, as well as my own, gives me satisfaction.

Favourite Walks.

1. The Wrekin. So many memories from childhood through to today especially back-to- back and back-to-back-to-back etc. gearing up to our annual challenges. Stunning views, being in nature and sense of achievement each time you touch the trig point.

2. Different Walks: new routes/new groups/inter-group walks/annual challenges/visiting various parts of the country and meeting other Group members/leaders I would not have normally met.

3. Invitation/event: Honoured and humbled to be part of 'Cameron Grant Memorial (Night) Walk'/supporting our curator, Daniel Reid, carrying the 'Baton of Hope' for 'Suicide Awareness and Prevention'.

My Mental Health Qualifications.

Mental Health First Aid England 'MHFA Level 2'.
Centre of Excellence - 'Mindfulness Diploma - Merit'.
NCFE Cache 'Certificate in Awareness of Mental Health Problems - Level 2'.
TQUK 'Self-Harm & Suicide Awareness & Prevention - Level 2'.

My Work Experiences.

'Mental Health Committee' member. 'Enable Network Committee' member. 'Well-being and Engagement Champion': sharing best practices, listening to staff, visiting team huddles. Empathy given to vulnerable customers. DDPYogi. Self-care advocate. Unofficial Oddballs and Prostate Cancer UK Ambassadors.
Mo-Bro (Movember participant for 10 years including being team captain).

My Real-Life Experiences.

Imposter syndrome. Generalised anxiety. Bullied. Bruised ego. Rejection. Loss. Trauma. Anger. Fear. Loneliness and isolation. Depression. Sensitivity. Burnout. Low work self-esteem. Low self-worth and confidence. Body dysmorphia. Self-sabotage. People-pleasing. Neurodiversity. Hyper-focus vs. procrastination and perfectionism. Creativity.

Lee Thornton
Essington Walk Leader

After 15 years of battling with drug addiction and the alcoholism, watching friends lose battles with inner demons while losing friends and family because I couldn't verbalize what was going on in my head. I decided enough was enough and spent the next 5 years fighting the fight and coming through the other side thanks to the support around me.

Fast forward to Nov 2023 and the build up to Remembrance Sunday, while doom scrolling through twitter I started to spot posts of people I had served with that had lost their battles, add to that the road adjacent to my house being closed twice due to 2 different people seeing no way out and leaping from a motorway bridge enough was enough and I had to do something/anything to help people.

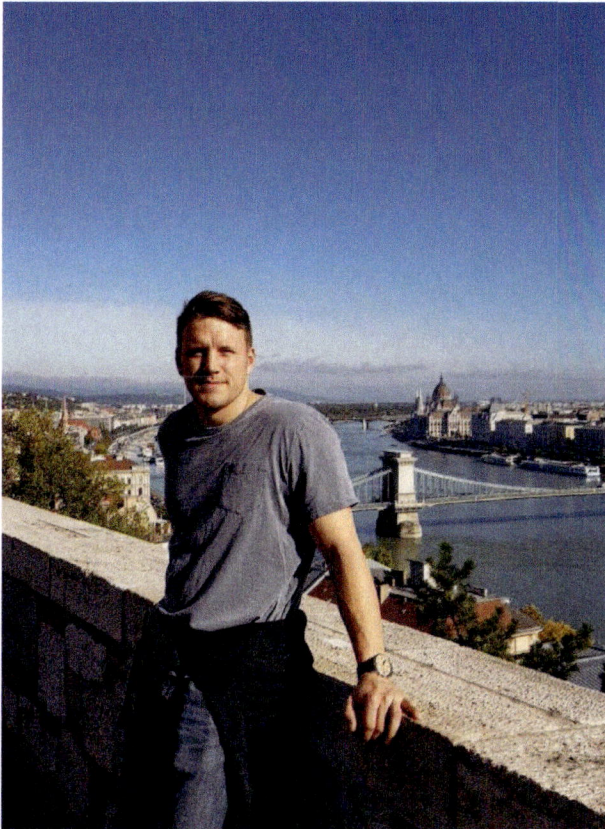

Now I fly the flag for Men Walking And Talking group for those who want support because of the magic it provides. It offers a sense of clarity and peace that people often struggle to find in the chaos of daily life. Each step allows us to release the weight of those thoughts and emotions that can build up while creating space for reflection and healing. In those moments outside, surrounded by nature and brothers in arms, we reconnect with ourselves and gain perspective. Walking transforms anxiety, stress and unrest into calm and reminds us that we are moving forward, one step at a time, toward a better state of mind while sharing experiences proves you're not along and we will be with you and if need be, drag you out the other side to a better and brighter future.

Danny Smith
Solihull Walk Leader

Up until the age of 32, life was good, everything was happy; things were going in the right direction. I was married, I had not long had the privilege of becoming a father and I felt confident in myself.
Come the year 2015 and everything went west. The relationship with my wife had all but broken down, I was living in a city I didn't like, in a job I hated, away from my friends and family and by the time Christmas of that year came about, we decided to separate.

It was fairly amicable, we both felt the same way but having a child that was 18 months old, we felt the need to fight for it longer than we should which lead to more arguing. The years to follow became the darkest, scariest, and most worrying of my life. It was at this time, I doubted myself more, I felt more alone, I didn't look after myself like I should have, I had no money but was lucky enough to start a job that eventually a few years down the line became my saviour. The big thing though was... I had no idea what to do about it.

Having visited my local GP, I found that to be equally as useless. There was more of an urge to put me on medication, when all I needed was someone to pour my heart out to. I needed someone to say "I know exactly how you feel mate, It sucks doesn't it!" and agree with me, instead of telling me what to do.

As I said, the job I landed enabled me to earn money to rebuild my life and get things back on track, but the consequence of those two dark years after the separation has forever been a burden on me.

I feel I manage my mental health well now, but I will have moments every year when my mind goes wandering and I fall back down the rabbit hole. I've thankfully learned a lot from my experiences which has made me stronger, but we're all human, and we all get impacted negatively at times, and I too have some low periods.

2024 saw a really big dip for me, as the summer went on and my financial situation was bothering me, my mind started to slip and things felt really bad once again. Now living in Solihull I decided to see what the local authorities could do to help which unfortunately did not come up successful. Being a talker, I wanted to talk. Being the headstrong person I am, I didn't want to be influenced by medication, but once again I felt what I needed didn't exist.

Until I was told about Men Walking And Talking...

A friend used MWAT previously and had loads of great things to say about his time with the group. Being quite an energized person, walking and talking... That's right up my street! Until I found that the nearest one was some distance from mine.

In my professional career, I am a manager of departments, a leader of people, a coach of 20+ years, a volunteer for the RAF Association and a Mental Health First Aider... Why not set up a walk of my own?

I'm a firm believer in "If you want a job doing properly, do it yourself" and given my life experiences and my professional skills... This is why I walk! We have an ever growing group in Solihull that's filled me with joy since it started, we are being backed by the council which is incredible support, and having launched in autumn knowing the winter period is a tough time for some gents, everything feels like it's fallen into place very nicely, and conveniently.

For the first time in a while, I'm experiencing something that I've not had for a while; Pride. Proud of the gents who make it out each week. Proud we are being trusted with other people's challenges in the hope we can support. Proud of my local council for doing all they can to make it a success. Proud of all the people on social media liking, commenting and sharing my posts. Proud of all the females who have made contact about their husbands, boyfriends, sons and brothers who need our group and finally... Proud of myself for wanting to change the world, one walk at a time.

We have a thing on our walks which has become a feature conversation -

"If there is one thing you can do between now and the next walk, that improves your mind-set by 1% and helps you feel one step ahead of where you are now... That is your plan for the week"

It's this mind-set that we're using so everyone knows that improving yourself isn't about making everything right at this moment, it's about making everything right eventually... 1% at a time.

Jason McCrae
Warwick Walk Leader

My story,

I work in the construction industry supply chain and due to one thing or another found myself being made redundant, I felt low and unworthy but pushed on and was offered a new position a few days later. A month into new position, guess what it happened again, twice in three months!

Here's where I changed, it absolutely battered me, could not get out of bed didn't want to wake up and felt a letdown to everyone around me. The thoughts I was having about not being here anymore just made it worse. I don't have the strength to carry on, my thoughts turned to how I was going to end it all.

I wasn't me anymore and who would want me (my thoughts) I spoke with my wife about how I felt and she was basically on 24hr watch checking in on me throughout the day whilst I was at home, hiding all medications/tablets - anything that I could harm myself with.

Finally got another job which is my current job but I struggled to engage and be enthusiastic about it and anything else. My wife spoke to a friend about a group she had seen in Kenilworth, MWAT group and that I should go, that was a big fat no from me when my wife suggested it.

Her friend then spoke to me directly and basically told me off, I then decided to go that week. Reluctantly I turned up in the car park and just sat there, Mark looked over so I was kind of forced to get out.

Here's where my life changed.

I walked up to Mark, he said are you Jason? I said yes and subsequently broke down. We chatted and met some of the others and went on the walk. I have to say we spoke about completely random stuff as we walked around and I felt loads better.
Mark and the group made me feel normally again.

I took the plunge to go on the zoom call on a Tuesday with Lee A and again broke down online in front of 8 guys, I was a mess but Lee made it ok. He pointed me in the direction of the lighthouse charity for counselling.

I have been at the Kenilworth group nearly a year and it has saved my life. I had some very difficult things to deal with but the whole MWAT community has helped me through it.

I have just completed my mental health first aider course and am actively helping others, time to give back.

I could have just give up and not been here anymore but MWAT was there.

Chapter 4
The guys!

Richard Green

From winter '22 through to spring / summer '23 I watched weekly Facebook posts about a bunch of chaps that met every Thursday evening in Kenilworth. They seemed to have camaraderie and a connection with each other that I began to envy. They seemed to be led by a guy who was infectiously positive, had a beaming smile and who pitched for new members to come and try. There would be no commitment expected, no judgement given, no cost, no talking unless willing. A seed was planted in my head.

The inner me kept justifying why I didn't need this, why they didn't need me and why I wouldn't really enjoy it anyway. Ever reluctant to step outside my comfort zone, which co-incidentally in reality can actually be quite uncomfortable, I continued to watch from afar, from the safety of my phone screen.

One week something changed. I picked up the phone and contacted Mark. He welcomed me to come and join the Kenilworth MWAT group that evening, 7pm at Abbey Fields car park and to my surprise I actually went. I was welcomed and as a group we spent the next hour and a half walking a 3/4 mile loop around the town. I chatted to several chaps who were all positive to see me. At the end of the walk I was invited to join the Kenilworth MWAT WhatsApp group that allows the connection of members to continue between the times of walking. Again I was assured that any participation with the group was not mandatory but at the individuals choice.

And so I went back. On week two I was no longer the new guy. I was welcomed with genuine affection. I saw other new people join who were probably now feeling some of the nerves that I felt on my first week. I did my part to reassure them and welcome them as I had been welcomed. The week's flowed, new faces were seen. There was a core group of people who turned out every week and then a bunch that came along as other demands on their time allowed.

The job that I had at the time did not give a fixed schedule and the hours were long. I could therefore not guarantee to be available on a Thursday evening to participate in MWAT. I became more and more disillusioned with my job, as the hours were brutal, I did not enjoy it and it was preventing me from doing something that I did enjoy. I also went through a relationship breakdown at the same time as my growing frustration with work. I had a eureka moment, let's say!

I quit work. I said to myself, "I will no longer be a puppet to anybody, be it either an employer or a partner. If either relationship is not giving back to me positively then I'm out".

Life is short, and sometimes we get stuck on the hamster wheel that burns our time. We look back and see a life unfulfilled and at times unhappy.
There was risk involved but then I thought something work wise will turn up. Continuing as I was, was no longer an option so I forced the issue.

I was now in a position to prioritise MWAT, and work and any future relationship would have to work around it. That's how important MWAT has become for me. I have since found alternative work that fits and as regards a relationship, well that's on hold for the moment.

I have learned that I need good and honest male friendships. I have life experiences and have come through some challenging situations, and am willing to help others, should the need arise. I will only know that need exists by being a committed and on-going active member to this great group.

I feel empowered to have made the commitment to MWAT, and to make other things in my life fall in line. I have only done so because I was welcomed and made to feel that I was part of something significant and that I truly belonged. It is now my responsibility, as I see it, to extend the same welcome to others.

Phil Clarke

I suppose my mental health journey began back in school, although I didn't know it at the time. It was a difficult time where I never knew where I fit in and there were a few years of bullying. I never knew how to stand up for myself so I just let it continue and it made me more and more unhappy. When I left in 2003 and moved in to work in the hospitality industry I began to enjoy life, made some good friendships and I forgot the bad times previously. I moved around a lot over the next couple of years and changed jobs into motorcycle sales. This is when the unhappiness came back; I had moved out from my parents' house and felt alone in the shared house I was in with no one to talk to. I remember crying a lot as it was the only way I could think to get out any emotion.

When I moved back in with my parents, I was able to get myself back on track and in 2009 I met my now wife and we made a plan to move to Lake District or close by, There were many hiccups on the way and I experienced bullying in an adult environment and more job unhappiness and I put my poor mental health down to this. But with our plan to move I had a purpose and we did it in 2016. After making a poor job choice to begin with I found myself a job that I still do today and I thought that I was "cured" because I didn't have any worries anymore. Then I became a Father and the pressures that it brings I found myself crying more, having more breakdowns, and incredible peaks and troughs of emotion. I began to accept that I wasn't cured and I was always going to be like this which made me feel worse.

But in August 2024 my wife found the Penrith group of MWAT so I joined in with a walk in Penrith. Since then it has made me feel that I'm not alone, I'm not broken I just needed help or to talk things through and feel no judgement. I might not always be able to attend but I know it's there and I look forward to the meets as an escape, a therapy and a reason to make myself better.

Steve Beeston

I first took up walking during lockdown as needed to get out of the house and I found it improved my mental health.

In 2023 I saw an advert on social media about MWAT and saw there was a local group in Worcester so I contacted Neil the walk leader and he said to come along. I was nervous at first meeting total strangers but they made me so welcome. I really enjoyed it and went along as often as I could.

I now regularly attend the walks each week and look forward to catching up with the men each work and some good friendships have been made.

I have always had a passion for Mental Health and 4 years ago I became a Mental Health Ally at work to help people struggling and I recently became a facilitator for a Men's Mental Health forum in my workplace and knowing I can try and help men open up and talk more and break down those barriers. Which I way I am so please to be involved with MWAT and what they are doing to help men, to talk or form friendship.

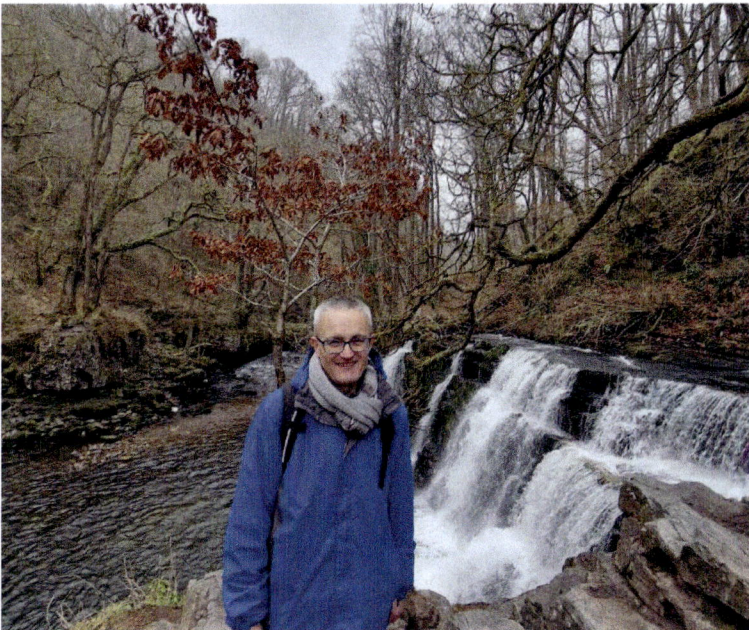

Dan Melville

Hi, I'm Dan from Crewe, Cheshire

I wanted to share my story as it's something I have only recently started, and ironically, I began around the same time the Men Walking And Talking group started in Sandbach. It's like it was fate!

It's always hard starting the conversation about depression and feelings, and that is no different for me as I try to write this story.

I suppose I'll begin with where things really changed, which was at the start of October 2024, when I finally admitted I had depression. To make this admission, I had to hit my rock bottom. My 17-year relationship at the time was on the rocks, and all it took was for a good friend to ask if I was depressed. This may seem so simple and obvious now, but at the time, it literally hit me like a train! I remember actually feeling something and not just numbness. It was a journey in itself in terms of emotions, as some of these feelings were things I had buried and hid away, never to think about again. I remember feeling liberated, which also felt weird considering the situation I was going through with my relationship. I had never been asked this before nor asked myself. I feel my depression started four years ago when I turned 30. I felt I was in a dead-end job with no direction. This was the lowest point of my life—I had suicidal thoughts, which I did try to act on but could never "pull the trigger," which also made me feel like a failure at the time.

It astonishes me that I still wouldn't have said I had a problem back then. I would never admit I was depressed, and that was the problem. I spent the next four years burying my feelings and shutting people out.

This changed the day I left home and finally admitted I had depression. Since then, I have been flooded with all the feelings I had bottled up for years. I found that speaking with my friends and family was the best thing I could have done. My issues stem from negative thinking, which then heightens my anxiety, and suddenly, that voice in my head doubts everything about me, it has literally put the brakes on my life. I am not letting it control me anymore!

Now I'm near the end of one chapter in my life, that book to be precise. I would be lying if I said I hadn't had thoughts of not wanting to be here anymore over the last month, but through resources like MWAT—which is an amazing support group for men of all ages and backgrounds—it's nice to know I'm not alone in this battle. I have already met some amazing guys who are living proof that I can beat this!

I've also realised the power of just talking with friends, no matter how stupid I feel it is. Feelings are feelings, and we all have them. No one's feelings are any more important than others, and I feel I'm a lot closer to my friends and family than I was before. I've started speaking with a therapist, which is still early days, but I feel it is beneficial and helps with reassurance that the work I'm doing on myself is okay. I have also done self- healing in terms of exercising and looking after my body, which in turn makes my mind a happier, more positive place. I am reading and studying mindfulness as well as writing in a journal daily—this is something I never thought I would do, but I actually enjoy it.

I know my book is closing from my previous life, but I'm so excited about chapter one in my next book. I want to be around for this book and see what I can do with this new chance at life. I no longer see myself as a coward or failure for not acting on those thoughts four years ago. Instead, I see myself as a strong-minded person who is ready for the next challenge that comes my way! I honestly believe that the majority of people suffer with mental health at some point in their life, and that's okay! I feel I've found a calling and want to get more involved in helping other people in any way I can. I'm only at the beginning of my journey and believe the journey will never end—should you ever stop trying to be a better version of yourself?

Chris Gardner

Men Walking And Talking

Especially talking,
As we're never meant to be that alone,
Human monkeys – social creatures,
Science proven we'll all go stir-crazy all alone in our people
boxes.

Remember granddaddy times years ago,
Where there was all that in-built social so you didn't,
Community, work socials, professional things, your local pub,
Not just ever more connected, but even less connected
somehow,
Just a mouth ineffectively screaming without noise,
In an endless uncaring noticing sea of people.

The toxic 21st century we've been given, is it a surprise
we're all losing it at a rate,
Take a pick add your own, cost of living sucked dry,
accommodation can't afford a shed,
Always on shifting sands, half a job each and your broken
pieces, no identity of your own,
Word, please talk to us, before you go justifyingly daft, just
go daft with company instead.

Better we talk and walk while we talk,
I get tired of it and so do you,
It's ok to not be ok and it's ok to be good too,
It's all a journey and we're all getting progress in some way,
There's always going to be the odd stone in your shoe,
It's good even if you don't think so,
The sun is there even if you can't see through clouds,
We're all a valid variation of that manliness we got told,
We're all brothers I say, and there's no shame in just you,
So let's all, Men walking and talking.

Smile

Go put on your plastic prepared face
And smile,
Because it is what everyone wants to see
Do you want like to, not your choice now,
Go quietly die inside.

Wonder if anyone knows to care,
Wonder if I can go tell broadcast,
Go through the masquerade parade,
Get up and present a perfect pose,
Cause this is what people like you to be,
And smile!

I blame, I don't know,
What happened,
All the lies I was told,
Every burden I was given,
Living with toxic times,
All put away now,
Because you are dictated,
That everyday has to be super-fine,
So you must,
And smile!

The Men of Salop

Andy, Arran, Richard, David, Adrian, Neil, Tony, Dean, Matt, Mathew, Kev. D, Chris, Robert, David, William, Steve. G, Martin. W, Martin. C, Keith, Foxy, Jamie, Stacey, Gazza, Simon. W, Steve. P, Declan, Dave, Paul, E, Nic, Paul. S, Simon, Dan, Del, John.

In Memory of Tyler

The men of Salop were the second group to be established in the Men Walking And Talking organisation and over the years many have come and gone but most have stayed and enjoyed the weekly walk along the River Severn and along the ancient defences of the town whilst talking and providing support for each other.

Amongst the many reasons for attending the walk the main theme seems to be around how the group gives the men an outlet to talk about their problems if they wish to but if not then they can lend an ear
to listen to someone else's problems. They share coping strategies that have helped them through personal experiences and struggles and there is no judgement by any member when hearing the stories of others.
They find it easier to talk to other men rather than family members due to a feeling of embarrassment. It provided solace for a member who had lost close family members and helped him take the first step to get his life back on track. The fact that they aren't the only person feeling like this and struggling makes them feel better.

After the walk they men report that they have the best night's sleep of the week after having the opportunity to offload any worries or upset they may have been feeling all week and the fresh air and exercise helps them keep active and healthy. They enjoy meeting some fantastic people old and new and developing friendships and a brotherhood all with a common goal of helping and being helped through that friendship and brotherhood. We have had thanks from men who report that the group have helped them through the hardest times of their lives and gave them a purpose to be here for the weekly walk. Every member commented that they were proud to be a member of Men Walking And Talking and proud of the achievements of the group and organisation as a whole.

R Wright

I have suffered on and off with mental health issues for as long as I can recall, mainly triggered by tumultuous relationships, culminating in a very difficult time in my career. I sought self-help a few years ago and although I do still have the odd 'dark day' in the main I'm feeling better about myself.

The group is really inspiring to me, to see how many similar experiences and challenges men face in life. I've worked in mental health support and it's been really insightful to pass on experiences, without 'telling' people what to do, I prefer to be there as a soundboard to offer face to face support, lend an ear to and if I can, ultimately give guidance.

Although the group is at an embryonic stage, it is clearly going in the right direction, which gives me a sense of pride to belong to. Long may it continue and flourish into other communities across the UK!

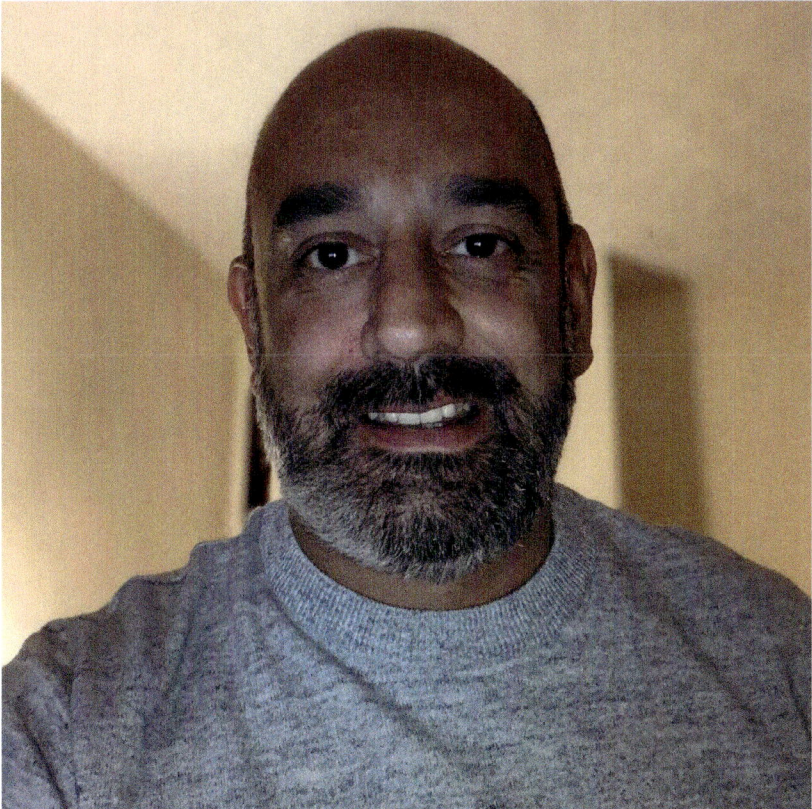

Binky Beaumont

Having hit mid 50's and having a partner that had life changing injuries in a road accident combined with losing my best friend of nearly 40 years last Christmas to cancer I was at a low point in my life, suddenly things that never mattered to me or ever bothered me before suddenly became a daily worry.

A few weeks ago I saw the MWAT post on social media, I thought why not?? But being older and not as fit as I was, my concern of it not being suitable for me were soon forgotten, I got such a warm friendly welcome from everyone that evening on week 3 and some great chats on all subjects, it was fantastic and making some new mates who were just walking and talking to each other each week is a welcome addition to my diary.

Even if the week and the world in general has not been as kind as you might hope and gets you down, just knowing there are other men feeling the same way about life and talking about feeling this way and meeting up in your area is a huge relief,

We are not alone and it's time for us all to talk and walk!!

Philip Haney

My recent move to Sandbach made me realise how difficult it can be when it comes to building new social relationships especially when you have recently retired.

It seems men find it harder to socialise than women do. Men worry about being judged or ridiculed for expressing emotions or engaging in deeper conversation. We often socialise around shared activities like sports or work-related topics. If their interests don't align, forming connections can be harder.

Modern cultural shifts might make men hesitant in initiating connections for fear of being misinterpreted or overstepping boundaries. Sharing personal struggles might seem as a sign of weakness

Creating activities such as walking to promote open communication can make a difference in the following ways:

Reduced pressure from face to face interaction.

Walking positions people side by side, which can seem less confrontational than sitting face to face. This set up makes it easier to open up, especially when it comes to the discussion of sensitive subjects.
The physical activity of walking provides a shared focus, reducing the intensity of the conversation and making silences or pauses feel less awkward.

Focus on the environment

Walking shifts part of the focus onto the surroundings, creating natural pauses and topics for conversation. This makes dialogue feel less intense or forced. I think men often appreciate this indirect approach

Time to Process Thoughts

Walking provides moments of silence that allow both parties to process thoughts. Men may appreciate this reflective space, making conversations during walks less rushed and more meaningful.

Reduced Social Pressures

By combining physical activity with dialogue in an informal setting, walking and talking provide a framework that feels natural and comfortable for men to deepen relationships.
I hope that the Sandbach walking and talking group provide an opportunity for people like me to listen and contribute in a safe space to end the stigma around men's mental health.

Chapter 5
Supporter stories

Jo

This is Mark's sister Jo.
We are a massively supportive family & not a day goes by
where we aren't in contact with each other either by phone
or WhatsApp. Over the years we have all needed support
from each other but I never would have thought that being
diagnosed with Breast Cancer December 2021 would have
led to seeing Mark become one of the directors of MWAT!
Talk about silver linings!

I only learned about this recently when listening to one of
Mark's many podcasts. I can, hand on heart say that MWAT
is Mark's calling in life! As a family we are so immensely
proud of seeing his weekly posts of the growing number of
men that turn up in Kenilworth & of all the extra work that
often goes on unseen. I know Mark doesn't really give his
brain chance to catch up with everything that has happened
in the charity as whenever there is a chance to promote or
widen the reach for vulnerable men he always says yes &
then figures out how it will work after!

I have leaflets in my bag all the time & will put them on any
notice boards I see. I always talk about MWAT at every
opportunity & I know my daughter's boyfriend has told her
that he & his mates were talking about the group & how
good it is for raising awareness. I know MWAT is here to stay
& I hope that it becomes a worldwide charity that gets the
recognition it so truly deserves.

Love to you all & keep being the amazing selfless heroes that
you are.

Oh I nearly forgot to say that it was such a pleasure to hold our Fundraiser this year for you guys. My mom has always supported Macmillan & various breast cancer charities but this year it was so special to see you all come together at our event & raise much needed funds.

The photo is where it all started!!

Lee Anderson

I've been a life coach for over 8 years now and I'm also an ambassador for a charity, Dan and I worked together and our relationship grew organically. Dan had started the Men Walking And Talking group, I approached him to see if he was interested in adding an online group that I was happy to facilitate and the online peer support group was born, providing a safe space for men to connect and talk.

I always looked forward to Tuesday nights because it was the online men's group. There was a good core to the group who show up every week and others would join when they needed to.

The group was facilitated by me but all of us were equal, we all had something to offer and it was important that was recognised by every member, no one was overlooked and everyone was made to feel valued and heard.

The group was very important to me because I live in a different country and didn't have access to any tangible English speaking groups.

Dan and I were talking one day and we decided to start the online group to give support to those who wasn't able to attend any of the walks or as well as.

I'm extremely proud to part of the group and if I'm honest I'm extremely gratefully to all the guys that gave me the space to talk about my issues.

The guys encourage openness and I know the group has probably saved a number of men from making decisions they may have regretted.

People need people and when they feel comfortable to share that can be what makes the difference.

Chapter 6
Testimonials

This is why we exist!

Below is a series of answers given as to "What does Men Walking And Talking mean to you?"

Cory Poynton: Being a part of the group has kind of helped me to socialise a bit better even though I still have bad social anxiety, it has made an impact even if it is the slightest.

Howard Wilson: The walk is the focal point of my week; it gives me a sense of being and belonging.

Chris Bark: Through the group I've found such wonderfully supportive friends. It has hugely helped me get through a very difficult episode in my life. Although there are a small few I chat to on walks but every one of them is great.

Darren Colledge: This group has truly saved my life. The support and genuine camaraderie from a mix of ages and backgrounds never ceases to amaze me.

Simon Rollason: It's great to be able to meet such interesting individuals and share experiences and support each other.

James Rajabali: It's a day I really look forward too. This group has got me through a very tough time in my life. I have met great people and we have supported each other through talking and listening. I have made great friends that I can talk about anything about.

Richard Green: MWAT is the focal point of my week. Other things fall in line behind it. I genuinely get excited during the journey in on a Thursday evening; prior to our 7pm meet. I want to be there for others and love the feeling of belonging, to a bunch of chaps who are infinitely stronger as a group than their individual parts.

Steve Windle: It was my first time last week, I'd followed the group on FB for quite a while and, after a particularly bad year, I finally came along and immediately felt at ease. I shared some of my troubles with Jason, and he told me some of his similar experiences, and I drove home definitely not feeling so alone. I'm really proud to become part of this group, not just for my own support, but hopefully to be able to support others should they need it. Thanks everyone.

Marco Cortese: I look forward to the walk, talk and company each Thursday. I've met some great people and made some good friends. It's good to catch up about anything and everything and share each other's experiences with support and advice along the way.

Jason McCrae: Finding and being part of this group I can honestly say has saved and changed my life. Not being wanting to be here anymore to being part of this supportive and caring group has changed my life. I could do this every night and now give back to those like me how need it.

Ashley Millington: MWAT walk gave me a weekly opportunity to maintain both physical and mental health, i found the group while rehabilitating from a major illness, it boosted both my physical and mental health at a time when both were rocky, forever grateful to be
a part of the group.

Rob Taylor: Doing this walk every Thursday the collective blokes that we've got is amazing all different backgrounds we all have each other's backs we all look after each other and when ones down we're there to get him back up for me the jokes the banter is like a family, which are thorough enjoy.
Martin Johnston-Smith: I can honestly say that this group although I've not been so active in the last few months has helped me get over some really difficult life changing events both in my work life and personally life and when I've had some of my lowest moments ever … and now i can say……I never been happier…what a turnaround! Thanks to you all, and a special call out to Darren.

Darren bates: What can I say this group is fantastic and changed my life for the better. I look forward to it every week and get serious FOMO when I can't make it. Love the relaxed atmosphere it gives and feel I can talk to anyone, it's especially helping me with the current situation with my wife's cancer diagnosis.

Ben: I find it helps to get active and engage other men in a safe & supportive environment, where everyone is valued and all can contribute as much or as little as they like. It definitely helps to be able to talk about mental health, or anything else that you want to, with others who understand and don't judge.

Paul Jenkins: The reason I decided to join the walking group is I didn't have a big circle of friends, and wanted to make new friendships with like-minded people. I struggle with my confidence and with my mental health. I know Ash through our kids being in the same class in primary school and now secondary school. Ash is a fantastic listener and always full of advice, but more importantly he's a great friend.

Dave: It's just an hour a week when I meet up with others who are in a similar place as myself, having had a few mental health issues over the years I find it helpful to just meet up and have the opportunity to talk about anything and everything without being judged, we all enjoy a good walk and also have the chance for a good laugh at times, but also discussing the current local affairs but also knowing that if there is something troubling our welfare we have someone who will be there for us to discuss it with

Lee: Camaraderie, Its ok, not to be ok

Neil: Meeting other guys and getting the reassurance that my feelings are normal.

Gaz: Safe space, being amongst others who may understand how you're feeling at times.

David: Lost a dad at my daughter's school to taking his life. Nobody could see it. So for me I wanted to step forward, lead from the front, be open to sharing and show strength in communication and owning my troubles but also moving forward with them.

Andrew: A weekly opportunity to accept your current self, embrace your future self and unlearn old ways of how society told you to behave/what social media told you that your life should be. A safe non-judgmental space to be your imperfectly perfect authentic self in a community you have created, that life has ignored until it was too late. We make the difference, we give glimmer of hope and we save lives.

Danny: My main objective of starting a group in my town was to provide a platform that I wished was there locally when I needed it. It makes my past and story worthwhile and brings me peace and closure. Being a walk leader gives me a sense of inclusion and acceptance. By far the best decision I have ever made and has been life changing.

Faz: Support, brotherhood! Opportunity to get shit out and how you actually feel maybe with somebody who kind of understands what you're going through what you been through and where you going to come out? Mostly, you're not alone!!! There is help and support sometimes from where you least expect. And this shall too pass!
Stevie: I'm obviously new here but I feel like soon I'll be able to echo a lot of that. My main goal in setting one up is to give blokes an environment or a space to feel like they can be, whether they open up and talk about what they're going through, or whether they just come for a walk and have some company for an hour a week. I think it's important for men to feel like they're not on their own when they're going through something, even if they choose to keep it all to themselves. So that's the main reason I'm here and I'm getting fat so I need to walk more.

Scott: Community connection, being there for others, getting to know new people.

Chapter 7
National events

Three Counties Walk 2022

In August 2022, Dan Reid and Andy set out to walk over 90miles in just three days in a mammoth fund-raising effort. Supported on all three days by Arran in the 'support car', as well as walking with numerous MWAT members along the way.

This was the first of what is now an annual fundraiser for Men Walking And Talking, growing in numbers year on year.

Yorkshire Three Peaks 2023

Over the weekend of 9th - 10th June 2023, 19 incredible men from across the country took on The Y3P challenge. 3 mountains, Pen Y Ghent, Whernside & Ingleborough with a total distance of 26 miles and over 5,000ft/1500m of ascent. It just happened to be one of the hottest days of the year too!

Setting off from our basecamp at 06:30 we knocked over the Pen-Y-Ghent in less than 2 hours.

We then had a 10 mile walk across stunning terrain to meet up with our support vehicle to replenish supplies, have a short rest and some food.

Onwards to Whernside, this for a lot turned out to be a challenging few hours in ever increasing heat. With a lot of mental battles overcome, a lot of grit and determination, we summited at approx. 16:00.

Onto the final ascent, Ingleborough, the approach to this took us across boardwalk paths and the looming steps to our final goal.

Those steps were soul crushing when they came into view, they seemed to snake their way up and up with no visible end. But, end they did and before we knew it, we had hit the summit for an epic group photo, lots of hugs and handshakes.

All that was left was to descend and return to the campsite! A signpost told us it was 4 miles!! Trust me when I tell you, it is a lie! That last leg back to base seemed to go on for an eternity, but with a mantra of one foot in front of the other until the end is reached, we rolled, some hobbled and limped into camp. Another round of hearty handshakes and hugs, before a well-earned beverage, or two!

All in all, an incredible day out on the hills with an absolute bunch of legends. The camaraderie shown during the day, especially when people were struggling or needed medical help (blisters and exhaustion) was great to see and typifies what Men Walking and Talking is all about.

Shropshire Summits 2024

On Saturday 7th September 2024, a group of men took on a challenging hike across the Shropshire Hills to raise money for Men Walking And Talking.

Starting at 06:50 and finishing at 18:28 they covered 22 miles and ascended over 3,500ft. They began the day in very challenging foggy conditions, which made for an interesting few hours to say the least. After ascending The Shooting Box, they then descended into Carding Mill Valley and on through Church Stretton to take on Caer Caradoc Hill, after a much needed rest they pushed on.

At the first arranged pit-stop in Cardington, changes were made to the pre-planned route due to lost time on the hills in the morning due to bad weather. By late afternoon the team was back on track and made it to the 2nd pit-stop.

They then all took on the last, hugely challenging stage from Little Stretton back to camp in Rattlinghope. This last stage was mostly uphill and took them to the summit of Pole Bank and on to complete the hike.

Back at camp and after many handshakes and pats on the back, the team all enjoyed a refreshing beverage or two. Very well deserved. Congratulations to all of the walkers and thank you so, so much to Andy and Arran for their support during the day and evening. Best vegetable soup ever!

One of our directors, Mark recalled his thoughts... "During the course of the day I witnessed many acts of support and brotherhood, which typifies what this organisation, stands for. Supporting your fellow man in times of need. For some of the guys that took part in this hike, it was a great personal challenge, walking distances and climbing up hills that they had never before attempted and they did it all with a smile on their faces (most of the time anyway). On the last section of the day, it became more of a mental battle than a physical one and yet again, everyone rose to the challenge."

Malvern Hills Inter Group Walk 2025

On Saturday 11th January 2025, 30 men gathered on a car park in Malvern, a large percentage of them had, until this day, never met in person. They came from many towns across the country, towns where we have weekly men's walking groups. It was a great chance for us to meet each other and spend a day walking over The Malvern Hills. We set off at 10:30 and headed toward the mist covered hills. Spirits were high as we left the main roads and started to ascend the steeper roads leading to the hills. We soon left these roads behind and found ourselves on well walked footpaths, after about a mile the terrain opened up to give us the most stunning view of a cloud inversion that stretched for miles. I think it is safe to say that every one of us was quite taken with this sight. After a brief stop for many photos we pressed on around the back of North Hill, where out of the sun, the temperature dropped, which pushed us on to find the sun again around the other side of Table Hill. We took a short break at about 2 miles in and spent some time admiring the incredible scenery, taking group and taking on refreshments.

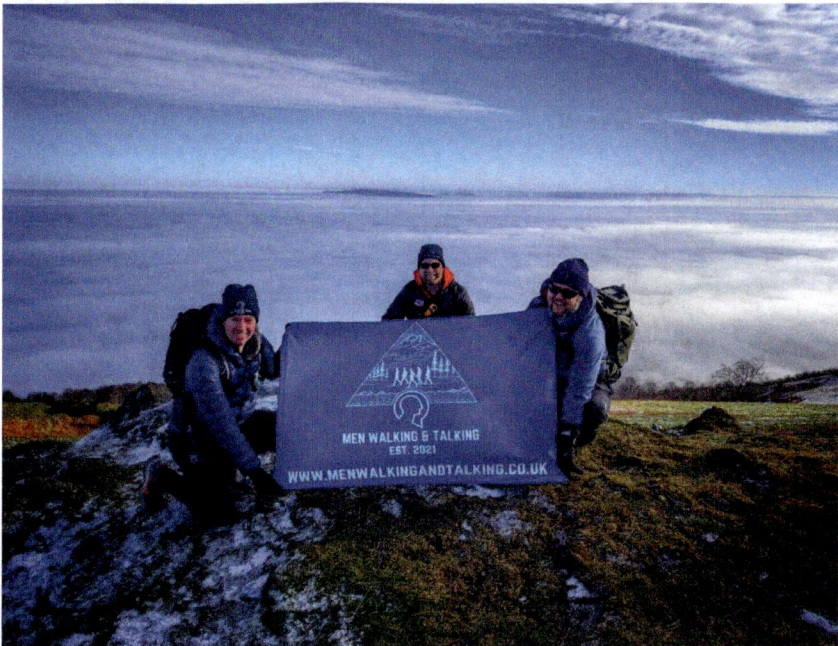

On we pushed, in and out of the sun, up and over Sugarloaf Hill and then finally the push to the main summit and highest point in the county, The Worcestershire Beacon.

The views from the top were quite simply breath taking. We found some places to sit and all broke for some well-deserved lunch. After lunch we all set off down to make our way for a well-earned libation. We were treated to some competitive downhill running from our military contingent, which hilariously nearly ended up with them both going A over T! They survived and we all had a good laugh. A great walk down off the hills and back into town, soon found us at our final destination for a refreshing drink, food for some and great conversations all around.

The camaraderie we witnessed as directors was nothing short of astounding, friendships made in an instant, forging new partnerships for walks to come!

Cameron Grant Memorial Trust

As an organisation we are delighted to be part of the Cameron Grant night walk, attending for the last few years, supporting this wonderful charity.

Cameron's Night Walk is typically on the Friday in October closest to 10 October, Cameron's birthday and World Mental Health Day. It is a relatively short event (7.2km / 4.5 miles) starting from and finishing in Hampton-in-Arden. The aim is to get as many people out and about as possible and to meet as many Night Walkers as possible afterwards in the Fentham Hall for refreshments.

Men Walking And Talking were hooked at the atmosphere of the event and the story resonates with us, we have since been back to support the walk as marshals and safety walkers to ensure the walk goes as smoothly and seamlessly as possible. Below is an extract from the website to give you an insight into why they do what they do.

Cameron took his own life in November 2014 aged just 21. He suffered from the symptoms of depression for seven years before he died, but managed to hide this from his parents and everyone who knew him. He seemed very happy at university and was planning to do a master's degree. Outwardly he was always smiling and was always the one who was there to cheer everyone else up.

We've learnt a lot about suicide since Cameron died, and the statistics are frightening. About ¾ of suicides are male and it is the biggest cause of death in the UK for boys and men under 50. 1 in 10 young people, or about 3 in every school classroom, are experiencing mental health problems at any given time and many people suffer in silence, as our son did. In 2013, there were 1769 road fatalities in the UK (roughly 5 a day), but more shockingly 6233 suicides (17 a day). There are many thousands more suffering from depression, self-harm and eating disorders.

To mark Cameron's life we established the Cameron Grant Memorial Trust in his name. The Trust is registered with the Charity Commission (see this link for details CAMERON GRANT MEMORIAL TRUST) and has Registered Number 1167221. Our Charitable objectives are:

The preservation and protection of good mental health in particular in young people by:

Raising awareness of young suicide
Urging all who are suffering in silence to speak up and ask for help
Supporting all who are fighting to overcome poor mental health, especially young people, and especially where this can be done through outdoor activities like hill-walking and Duke of Edinburgh's Award
Assisting in the provision of education and support that will help to increase awareness and knowledge of the issues around mental health and well-being for all and especially amongst young people

We want to eradicate stigma and create a sea-change in attitudes to mental health in the UK. In our lifetimes, attitudes have changed dramatically towards smoking, drink-driving, sexual equality, same-sex partnerships and many other social issues. We want to do the same for mental health. We want to play our part in preventing suicides, but as importantly, persuade people to reach out for help before they reach a crisis point.

Because Cameron suffered in silence our main approach is to encourage all who are in any mental distress to speak up and ask for help. We do this by creating "signposts" with help information. Our signposts might be the drinks mats we call Cameron's Coasters, wellbeing postcards, business cards or any other physical item on which we can print help information. We customise our signposts so that they have the help information most important for the setting where they are used. As of Oct 2024 we have produced over 1.4 million Coasters and more than 230,000 postcards and business cards, and they are in use across the UK.

We offer this personalised signposting free of charge and can only do this because of the generosity of those who make donations to us and fundraise for us. We are not funded by local or national government, or by any part of the NHS.

In addition to creating signposts, we make small grants to support mental health innovation and to support other mental health charities. In 2024 we made two grants totalling £23,000 to provide counselling support for young people in Solihull and Birmingham.

Poor Mental Health can affect anyone and there is no shame in having an illness, physical or mental and seeking help for it. We hope that by spreading this message openly and honestly and providing support to young people through the Trust we can help many others in Cameron's memory. We miss Cameron an unbelievable amount and we so wish that he had asked for help.

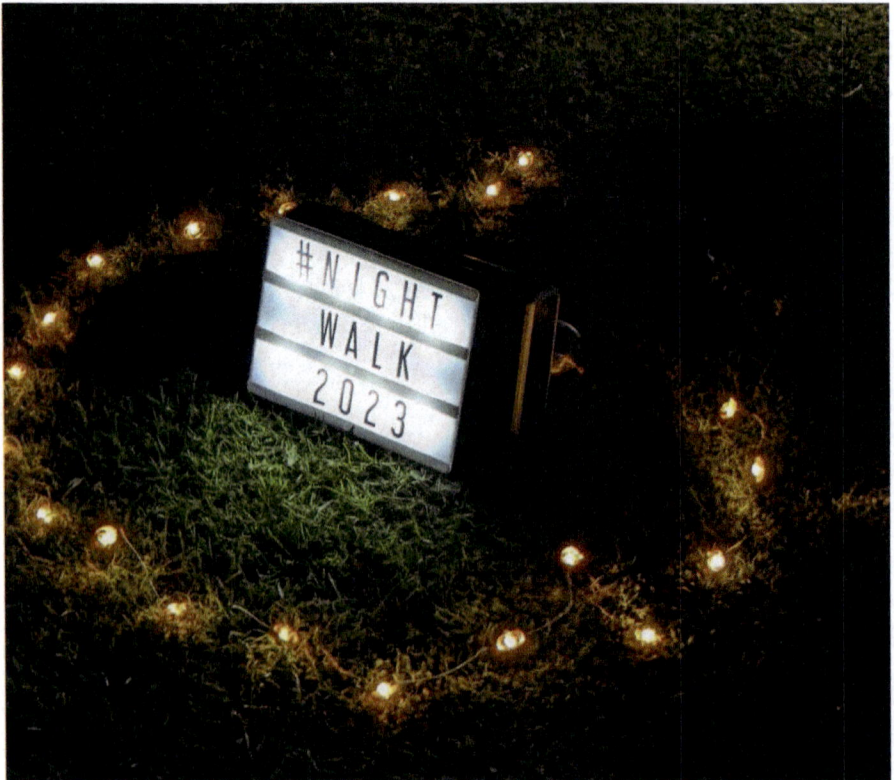

The Armed Forces Covenant

Philip Sinclair, Regional Employer Engagement Director said:

"Mental health in men has long been a taboo subject, kept in the shadows, but thankfully now emerging. In doing so, however, the scale of what confronts us as a society is becoming increasingly evident, reaching pandemic proportions. Whilst not an infectious disease, it nonetheless has a similar impact, causing loved ones, friends and family to become separated, unable to meet, or in this context, talk. The seemingly innocuous past time of men walking and talking together therefore takes on a much more significant purpose, encouraging individuals struggling to come to terms with their mental health and unable to talk about it with their loved ones; to instead do so with strangers on a similar journey. By confronting the spectre together, they are hopefully able to leave the shadows, and find themselves in a better place.

I am honoured to have been approached by one of the contributors and asked to write this forward. Men Walking And Talking are in the vanguard essentially of emerging support networks aiming to provide that 'safe space' to help improve mental health and wellbeing before it becomes an overwhelming problem for individuals to deal with.

Ash and I have crossed paths professionally several times, working in and around the Armed Forces Covenant. Early in their foundation, Men Walking And Talking became signatories to the Covenant, and I am delighted that they have done so, publically acknowledging their support for the Armed Forces Community. Mental health however is not confined to single communities, it has no boundaries, and spreads across multiple communities all over the world. A pandemic indeed. 'Why we walk' is for everyone, and the contributors come from all walks of life, illustrating the impact across all communities. I commend it to you.

Early in 2024 our directors came together for a meeting to discuss how we can support the Armed Forces community, it had become apparent that the groups have a pretty even split of armed forces connections and those without, some of whom have needed specialist assistance at some point in their mental health journey, so a decision was made to sign the Armed Forces Covenant.

The Armed Forces Covenant is a promise by the nation ensuring that those who serve or have served in the Armed Forces, and their families, are treated fairly.

We have a few individuals with military charity experience and specialisms within the field, so it was an easy decision to get involved, with the aim to host specific Armed Forces walks for those who are not able to attend our regular walks, giving an opportunity they may not have had prior.

The covenant was signed on 2nd May 2024 with Commandant of No1 Flying Training School & Defence College of Air & Space Operations, and was a huge privilege. We commit to honour and support those in the community recognising the value of our Forces, both Regular and Reserve, Veterans and Families, something we consistently do without question.

Family & Friends Walks

Here at Men Walking And Talking we are well aware of the value of family and friends, so its highly important that we involve as many of our family and friends when possible. Back in 2023 our first family and friends took place in Carding Mill Valley, Shropshire. With over 30 people attending in glorious sunshine we followed the way marked route up along the meandering stream to Lightspout Waterfall, a four metre natural water feature Victorian visitors called a "miniature Niagra". Following a quick stop for photos and playing in the waterfall to cool down we traversed around the Long Mynd for a family picnic and back down with a diversion to the reservoir, notorious for wild swimming! It was so great to see so many having a dip, some for their first experience of cold, wild swimming and so many smiling faces as we headed back for an ice cream! Memories that will last forever!

2025, February, snow covered hills, thick fog and freezing temperatures sets the scene for the second Men Walking And Talking family and friends walk. Deep in the Bannau Brycheiniog (Brecon beacons) lies some spectacular scenery, not that we could see it at first. We all met next to the Porth yr Ogof, translated to the gateway of the cave for our pre walk brief, a perfect opportunity for a photo, it was instantly recognisable that this group were going to be great – so much chatter between them straight away, some had travelled over 120 miles to be with us and others more local. We set off along the narrow, winding path along the Afon Hepste River, jumping fallen trees and smaller tributaries until we met the main path to our first waterfall, the Sgwd Clun-Gwyn (upper "fall of the white meadow"). The beauty of the route takes in the smaller falls to start and build up with the Sgwd Isaf Clun-Gwyn (lower), Sgwd y Pannwr (fall of the fuller" to the most spectacular of the day, the wonderful Sgwd yr Eira (The waterfall of snow) with a thunderous roar as the water falls to the pool below with some of the group taking in a breath taking view behind the curtain of water. Parts of the walk, mainly the steep decline and incline to the upper and lower falls, added to the challenging conditions of mud and damp rocks gave the younger members of the group a huge sense of pride for completing the near 6 miles, however the biggest challenge for us all was the 190 steps down, and 190 steps back up from the final falls, but I think we all will agree the burning calves and aching backs are well worth it for the day we had!

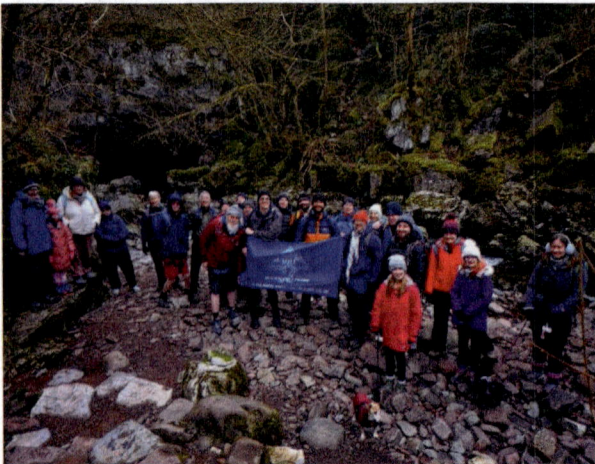

Supporting others

Men Walking And Talking are regularly approached to support other events around the country, and so many of those are similar organisations, with similar goals. Some of those requests are for social media interaction, interacting with podcasts, promoting to charitable and corporate organisations or providing walk leaders to support with physical events. Whilst we cannot support all requests we endeavour to support as many as possible.

Hike at Night for Mountain Rescue England & Wales (MREW) is a relatively new event organized by our friends at Adventure Buddies, an event that has a different challenge, walking in complete darkness. In 2023 one of our directors, Ash attended the Pen Y Fan "Hike at Night" and found the community and atmosphere to be pretty incredible, setting off to catch the sunset at the summit with hundreds of other walkers (the weather was perfect) with smiles all round. Ash decided right then that he would be volunteering to assist if the event were to happen again. Months had passed and an advertisement was posted "Walk Hosts Required for night walk", instantly Ash decided he would offer his, his wife, Kelly and fellow director Mark's services to host a walk in 2024.

The walk started as the sun was setting, following a safety brief, communications check and essential head torch check, the group were very excited as many of them had never experienced a night walk. A night walk is very different to that in the daylight, even doing the same route can be very different in the dark, meaning navigation, communication and experience is essential. The group was blessed with a super moon for some spectacular views at the summit. With Mark leading, Kelly being rear marker and Ash as safety coordination from the car park the group completed the walk in about 3 hours with some excellent feedback and thousands of pounds raised for MREW.

Adventure Buddies

My journey started after a challenging period of poor mental health. During this time, I rediscovered my love for the outdoors, which became a vital part of my healing. Hiking and scrambling not only helped me find my footing again but also to rebuild my confidence and find renewed clarity.

The benefits of spending time outside, surrounded by fresh air and nature, are truly transformative. Regular exercise in natural settings has been shown to boost both physical and mental well-being, helping to relieve stress, lift mood, and enhance overall health. This connection with nature can remind us of the beauty around us and offers moments of peace and self-reflection that are hard to find elsewhere.

My passion for the outdoors quickly grew, but I noticed that many online groups were missing the warmth and encouragement I believed was crucial for fostering confidence and resilience. Driven to make a difference, I founded Adventure Buddies to be a supportive space where people could find their strength and embrace new adventures. As much as I and the admin team encourage getting outdoors, they are equally committed to promoting safety and supporting our Mountain Rescue teams. The essential work of Mountain Rescue England and Wales deserves our deepest gratitude, as they selflessly assist adventurers in times of need. We cannot thank our members enough for their incredible contributions to our fundraising efforts, helping to sustain these remarkable teams and ensure safety in our shared outdoor spaces.

Although awareness of mental health has grown, it remains a difficult topic for many to discuss openly. Recent tragic stories, including the loss of a young celebrity, remind us that there is still much work to be done. The media's and internet's treatment of his grieving family underscore the risks of our digital world. Here at Adventure Buddies, we're determined to be a safe haven—more than just a social media group, we are a community. We're here to lift each other up, to be there when life gets challenging, and to go on adventures with you, no matter your fitness level or confidence. We are here, together.

I am all too familiar what being present on social media can also bring. As high as you climb the ladder putting yourself out there, someone will always do what they can to bring you down. Regardless of any wrongdoing, lies, or undermining it takes to see you suffer or just to cause a negative impact on what you set out to achieve. Sayings like "you need to be thick skinned" are just so fake! These comments and doings hurt and make you consider all your good intentions "are they really worth it". My children and the support from Nicki make it all worthwhile, and will continue to show good will always prevail over hatred and evil. It just takes time, a lot of tears and the wanting.

Finally, we would like to extend our heartfelt thanks to Mountain Rescue England and Wales, as well as to each and every one of our members who have actively supported our fundraising efforts this year. Whether you participated in our night hike, attended this evening's ball, donated, or simply helped to spread the word, your generosity and spirit make all the difference. Without you, we wouldn't be the group we are today. Thank you for being an essential part of our journey and for helping us to make a positive impact in the lives of so many.

Woodland Xperiences

Men Walking And Talking have teamed up with Woodland Xperiences, who offer wellbeing support for our Armed Forces, Blue Light & Veteran community. We feel passionately about the outdoors and have a lot in common with Woodland Xperiences, showing passion to support those in need by using the great outdoors.

Woodland Xperiences profoundly believe in the therapeutic power of getting back to nature and utilising adventurous activities on both land and water, thriving on creating support packages and hosting a safe conversational environment to assist mental & physical health & well-being, isolation, moral belief & recovery. They are committed to helping those working within, and retired from the Armed Forces and Blue Light community.

The Woodland Xperiences Ethos

We all stare at the dancing flames, hypnotic as they are. If we could read them they would be telling their own stories and adventures!
Taking time out from the treadmill of work and life is fundamental in maintaining a balanced healthy mind and body. People from all walks of life experience traumas and conflict which can have a detrimental effect on our mental and physical health. Which in turn is then put to one side but boils away within us without us sometimes knowing, ready to explode at any trigger affecting close family, friends, relationships, work and unconsciously ourselves.

Building on and considering research, thoughts, and findings of others together with personal experiences of prolonged exposure to the outdoors, Woodland Xperiences was created, to assist with Post Traumatic Growth.

Men Walking And Talking have collaborated with Woodland Xperiences and other like-minded groups, across the country to help raise awareness about how we as a community provide support for mental health, wellbeing, life's challenges and suicide intervention. The photo below shows the directors of Men Walking And Talking at a recent visit to the National Memorial Arboretum.

The founder of Woodland Xperiences, Ady states this on their website,
Being outdoors and closer to nature is good for you, your mind, your business and your families.
We couldn't agree more!

Men Walking and Talking

Walking and talking beneath the sky,
A place where no man needs to hide or lie.

The weight we carry, we leave on the ground,
In steps and words, our healing is found.

Together we climb, not just the hills,
But mountains of silence, past pain and stills.

A bond that's formed with every stride,
No need for masks, just truth by our side.

It's more than a walk; it's a lifeline we share,
A force for good, for men who dare.

To speak their minds, to feel and be free—
This group has done that, not just for them, but for me.

It's a light in the dark, a hand to hold,
A space where our stories can all be told.

In a world where men's mental health is thin,
This group's a place where we can start to heal within.

© Dominic Braithwaite

Proceeds of this book go directly back into
Men Walking And Talking CIC

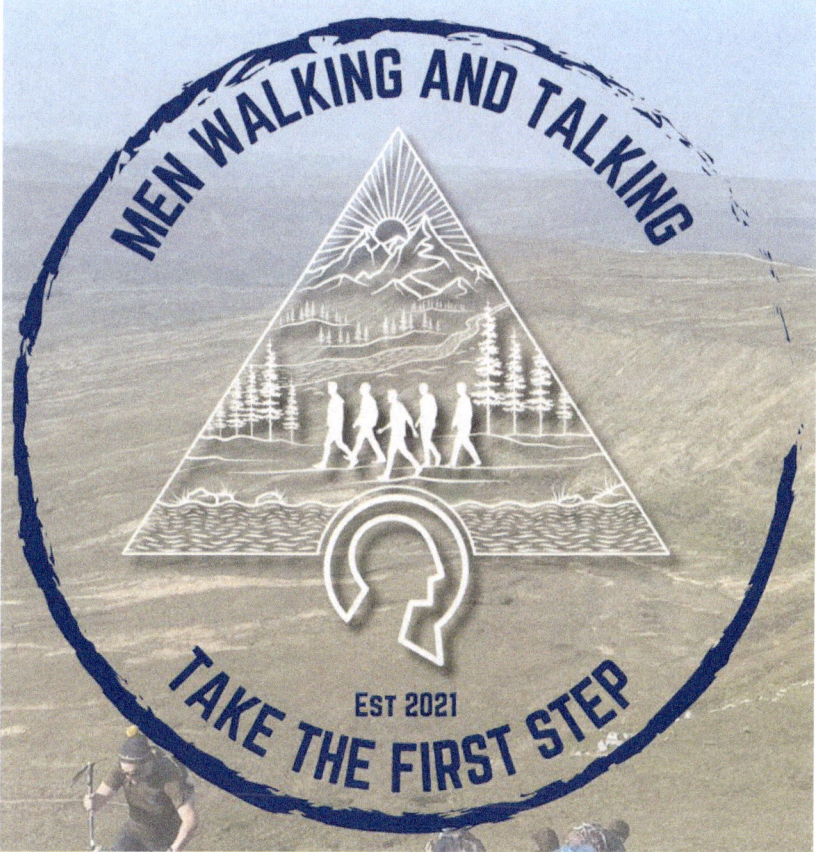

Thank you!

Printed in Great Britain
by Amazon

62786332R00097